LOOKING BACK AT TRADITIONAL CARGO SHIPS

by
Andrew Wiltshire

The *Jami* is a splendid example of a traditional cargo liner, hard at work tramping. She is seen heading up the Shatt-al-Arab waterway towards the end of her career, on the very hot and humid afternoon of 15 May 1980. The *Jami* is sailing for Irano-Hind Shipping Co Ltd (a joint venture between the Islamic Republic of Iran Shipping Lines and the Shipping Corporation of India) and is registered at Bandar Abbas, Iran. She was completed in 1957 by Blohm & Voss AG, Hamburg, as *Waterland*. As such, she was the final ship in a series of three built at this yard for NV tot Voortzetting van de Koninklijke Hollandsche Lloyd (Royal Dutch Lloyd) of Amsterdam. She was completed as an open shelter deck vessel, but in this view her layout had become closed shelter deck, giving her a revised gross tonnage of 9,413. She had accommodation for twelve passengers as well as providing some refrigerated capacity, and featured five cargo holds as well as tunnel side tanks for edible oils. Of special note are her unusually high masts, especially the king posts situated forward and aft. In 1972 she became *Iran Mehr* for South Shipping Lines, Iran, becoming *Jami* in 1977. On 18 December 1982 the *Jami* was hit by two guided missiles from an Iraqi aircraft while on a voyage from Chalna to Bandar Khomeini. She caught fire and sank in the Khor Musa Channel, another victim of the Iran/Iraq war.

(Andrew Wiltshire)

IINTRODUCTION

In this world of container ships and bulk carriers, the traditional cargo ship in 2015 is now but a distant memory on our oceans. It has been gradually phased out over the last fifty years or so by the modern efficiencies of containerisation and carriage of goods in bulk.

For the purpose of this book, a *traditional* cargo ship will be defined as a dry-cargo vessel that has cargo accommodation both forward and aft of its machinery space. Therefore, this will cover cargo ships that are termed mid-ships layout, three-quarters aft layout and also those with a split superstructure. We will take a look at cargo liners, former cargo liners and tramp ships in service under a wide variety of flags. Some ships date back as far as 1914 and we cover some of the classic designs that appeared through to the early 1980s. I would like to think that this book will bring back some happy memories for many, especially those readers who were lucky enough to sail on or work with traditional cargo ships.

Some abbreviations used throughout are: grt (gross registered tonnage), dwt (deadweight tonnage), TEU (twenty-foot equivalent unit), bhp (brake horse power), ihp (indicated horsepower), shp (shaft horsepower) and rpm (revolutions per minute).

Acknowledgements

Many thanks must go to Nigel Jones and Douglas Cromby for their encouragement in getting the project started. A big thank you must also go to all the other contributors including Trevor Jones, Paul Boot, Réne Beauchamp, Marc Piché and Kevin Blair for the time and effort they have willingly given to my requests for help.

I am particularly grateful to Malcolm Cranfield who has very kindly checked all the captions, and weeded out any errors that he found while at the same time making some valuable suggestions. Finally, as always, I am grateful to Bernard McCall for his support and Gil Mayes for checking the captions, and of course my wife Tracey for letting me embark on another shipping volume.

Written sources used throughout include copies of Ian Allan *Ocean Ships*, *Lloyds Register of Shipping* (various years), a number of World Ship Society publications, as well as several volumes of *Merchant Ships World Built* (published in years 1954-70).

Andrew Wiltshire   Cardiff   March, 2015

Front cover: London & Overseas Freighters Ltd (LOF) was founded in 1949 as a tramp-tanker venture by London-based Greek shipowners, Rethymnis and Kulukundis. Ten dry-cargo vessels transferred from Counties Ship Management were gradually replaced by new tankers and a bulk carrier, and between 1963 and 1965 London & Overseas Freighters took delivery of six modern dry-cargo ships. The **London Statesman** was followed by the **London Craftsman**, **London Tradesman** and **London Citizen** from the yard of Uddevallavarvet AB in Sweden. These were six-hold open shelter deck/closed shelter deck vessels of 531 feet overall length. The slightly smaller **London Banker** and **London Advocate** were completed in the Netherlands by NV Kon Maats "De Schelde" at Flushing as five-hold ships. The **London Banker** had in fact been launched in June 1963 at the Gorinchem shipyard of "IJsselwerf", being completed at Flushing in the November. She is seen here arriving at Avonmouth on the early morning tide of 10 February 1973 on her last voyage for LOF. She was then sold and became the **Riva** for Mina Corporation (T Tricoglou) of Piraeus. After being laid up at Galaxidi in Greece from May 1982, she undertook a single voyage to India in May 1986 as the Maltese-flagged **Alysia Bay**. From there she sailed to Chittagong to be broken up.

(John Wiltshire)

Back cover: A new series of six 16-knot cargo liners was introduced by Ellerman Lines in 1956 with the delivery of the **City of Colombo**. She was a motorship and was completed by Barclay, Curle & Co Ltd at Glasgow. The remaining five vessels were delivered from four other shipyards, being concluded with the **City of Auckland** in 1958 from Vickers Armstrongs (Shipbuilders) Ltd at Newcastle. This builder produced two ships in the series, the first being the **City of Ripon**, which was launched on 19 July 1955 at their High Walker yard. She was completed during March 1956 and delivered to Ellerman Lines Ltd (The City Line Ltd) and registered in Glasgow. She was an open shelter deck type vessel with a gross tonnage of 7,713 and had accommodation for four passengers. Her hull was 507 feet long and she had a beam of 65 feet. Five holds were served by seventeen derricks which included a heavy lift example of 70 tons capacity at No 3 hold. All six ships in this class were Doxford-powered and the **City of Ripon** was installed with a 6-cylinder version which developed 8800bhp. In this view the **City of Ripon** is on Britannia Wharf in Roath Basin at Cardiff, prior to sailing on 25 October 1971 to load for East Africa. She later became **Benvannoch** in 1978 for Ben Line Steamers Ltd, Leith, and arrived at Kaohsiung for scrapping on 20 April 1979.

(the late T W Wiltshire)

CLASSIC CARGO LINERS Elder Dempster Lines Ltd operated principally from ports in the UK, northern Europe, the Mediterranean and North America to destinations in West Africa. Completed in 1952 for the service from North America to South and West Africa were the larger 16-knot motorships **Eboe** and **Ebani.** They were both completed by Scotts' Shipbuilding and Engineering Co Ltd of Greenock and featured a long bridge deck. They were 508 feet in length, with some refrigerated capacity and offered accommodation for up to twelve passengers. The **Eboe** was the first completed in March 1952, having been launched the previous September. She had a gross tonnage of 9,380 and featured four cargo holds served by twenty derricks. They were later deployed on the UK to Nigeria run,

calling at Senegal and Ghana. In 1973 the **Ebani** came under the ownership of China Mutual Steam Navigation (Blue Funnel Line) trading to the Far East for about one year before returning to Elder Dempster operation, and eventual sale for scrap in 1977. The **Eboe** was sold to Triton Navigation Corporation (managed by Maldive Shipping Ltd) in 1977 as **Georgia** under the Panamanian flag. On 8 October she sailed from Gdansk bound for Mogadiscio, arriving there on 14 November. Maldive Shipping Ltd became her owners in January 1978 and she was delivered to shipbreakers at Gadani Beach the following month. In this view we see the **Eboe** arriving on the River Mersey in early July 1973 on a voyage from Douala via Belfast.

(Paul Boot)

The **Coromandel** was the second of two motor cargo liners delivered to the Peninsular and Oriental Steam Navigation Company for deployment on the Europe to India service. The first ship was the **Cannanore** completed in July 1949, with the **Coromandel** following her into service in October that year, and were based on British India's pre-war C-class design. Both were constructed at Whiteinch on the Clyde by Barclay, Curle & Co Ltd. The **Coromandel** had a gross tonnage of 7,065 and was powered by a 6-cylinder Doxford diesel of 6,800bhp built by the shipyard. She had five holds which included up to 20,710 cubic feet of refrigerated storage, as well as a deep tank situated aft. She had a complement of ninety-six officers and crew, and could also accommodate twelve passengers. After a few years both sisters were transferred to P&O's services from Europe to the Far East, and ports of call included Penang, Singapore, Hong Kong, Manila and Japan. The **Coromandel** is seen arriving on the River Thames in September 1968. She was the first of the two sisters to be sold, passing in 1969 to Jebshun Shipping Co Ltd as **Shun Hing**, initially registered in London and from 1971 in Singapore. While laid up at Manila in the Philippines, she was driven ashore on 25 June 1972 during a typhoon. Refloated two weeks later, she became the **Hop Sing** for a final voyage to shipbreakers at Kaohsiung in February 1973.

(Douglas Cromby collection)

The **President Taft** was a fast cargo liner of 14,764grt for deployment on the west coast of the United States Transpacific services. She was operated by American President Lines Ltd, of San Francisco, and was the third ship in the *Seamaster* class, being completed in December 1967. She was a product of the Ingalls Shipbuilding Corporation yard at Pascagoula, Mississippi, and this C4-S-69a class of ship incorporated a new high-strength low-alloy steel, which gave a weight saving of 18%. The **President Taft** could accommodate break-bulk, containerised, refrigerated and some liquid cargoes, and featured a transom stern to increase cargo capacity. She had a crew of forty-five and luxurious facilities for twelve passengers. Her main machinery consisted of two steam turbines by General Electric Co with an output of 24,000shp. This gave the vessel a range of 11,600 nautical miles at 23 knots. She is captured on film departing Los Angeles in June 1970. The distinctive sturdy-looking design of her cargo-handling gear is noteworthy. In 1972 all five ships in this class were lengthened and rebuilt into pure container ships for their owner, with a TEU capacity of 611. The overall length of the **President Taft** increased from 574 to 663 feet and her gross tonnage was now recorded as 17,342. She went on to give good service, and in December 1992 she passed to shipbreakers at Kaohsiung, where work began in early 1993.

(Marc Piché)

Glen Line Ltd was purchased in April 1935 by former rival on the Far East trade, Alfred Holt and Company. It was operated as a separate fleet and in 1967 had around fourteen cargo liners on fleet strength, five of which pre-dated 1942. The **Cardiganshire** is seen discharging at London's Royal Docks in June 1971, a good place to see Glen Line ships. The **Cardiganshire** was completed in October 1950 by Caledon Shipbuilding & Engineering Co Ltd at Dundee as **Bellerophon** for Ocean Steam Ship Co Ltd of Liverpool, and wore the colours of Alfred Holt's Blue Funnel Line. She was of 7,724grt and had an overall length of 487 feet, while her six holds were served by twenty-six derricks ranging from 5 to 50 tons capacity. The

main engine was a 7-cylinder Burmeister and Wain of 7,600bhp built by J G Kincaid & Co Ltd and gave a service speed of 16 knots. The **Bellerophon** was transferred to Glen Line in 1957 at which point some refrigerated cargo space was added. In 1972 **Cardiganshire** was transferred to China Mutual Steam Navigation Co Ltd (Blue Funnel Line) and regained her original name **Bellerophon**. She was sold out of the group in 1976 to Orri Navigation Lines (Saudi Europe Lines Ltd, Jeddah) as **Obhor**. She was broken up at Gadani Beach in November 1978.

(the late C C Beazley)

In 1956/57 the French shipping company, Compagnie Maritime des Chargeurs Réunis sold its three modern cargo liners, **Clement Ader**, **Edouard Branly** and **Henri-Poincare** which had been built for use on the Marseille to Indo China service, and featured accommodation for 91 first class, 52 second class and 398 third class passengers. They passed to Italian owner "Italia" Soc Per Azioni di Navigazione of Genoa, part of the FINMARE Group, who renamed them **Alessandro Volta**, **Antonio Pacinotti** and **Galileo Ferraris** respectively for service to America, and downgraded them to cargo ships with facilities for just twelve passengers. The **Antonio Pacinotti** was named after a well-known Italian

physicist and was completed in January 1953 by Ateliers & Chantiers de la Loire at St Nazaire as the **Edouard Branly**. Of 11,298grt, she was a twin-screw motorship powered by a pair of 8-cylinder Cie De Const Méc diesels of 11,200bhp. During the 1970s the ships were transferred to Lloyd Triestino's services to Africa and the Far East. In this view the elegant-looking **Antonio Pacinotti** is seen at Durban in about February 1974, by which time the ships were frequent visitors to the port on Lloyd Triestino's services. All three vessels were taken out of service in 1978, and broken up at La Spezia during the following year.

(Trevor Jones)

The Koninklijke Java-China Paketvaart Lijnen NV (Royal Interocean Lines) fleet based in Amsterdam was the first Dutch shipping company to take delivery of a Japanese-built ship, with the completion of the **Straat Futami**. She was classed as a high speed cargo liner and was completed at the Osaka yard of Hitachi Zosen in August 1965. In addition to general cargo she was designed to carry bulk cargoes such as ore and also some refrigerated cargo. The **Straat Futami** had a gross tonnage of 9,374 and featured a 13-foot long bulbous bow, while her speed was given as 19 knots. Hitachi Zosen followed by delivering the **Straat Fushimi** by the end of 1965 and **Straat Fiji** in early 1966. A fourth ship in this series was the **Straat Florida** completed by Nippon Kokan at Shimizu in June 1966. In 1968 these four ships were typically employed on sailings between Japan, Singapore, South Africa, Argentina, Brazil and returning via a similar route. In 1970 Royal Interocean Lines was merged with three other Dutch shipping companies to form Nederlandsche Scheepvaart Unie which, in 1977, was renamed Koninklijke Nedlloyd Groep NV (Royal Nedlloyd Group). The **Straat Futami** is seen from the south breakwater pier, Durban, in January 1974. She became **Nedlloyd Futami** in 1978 and was sold in 1980 to Char Ching Marine Co Ltd of Taiwan as **Char Mou** under the Panamanian flag. Just under four years later in January 1984, she passed to shipbreakers at Kaohsiung.

(Trevor Jones)

Blue Star Line Ltd, London, placed an order with Cammell Laird & Co Ltd of Birkenhead to construct four refrigerated cargo/passenger liners to replace vessels lost during WWII. The names **Argentina Star**, **Brasil Star**, **Uruguay Star** and **Paraguay Star** were allocated to these ships, and they were required to operate the service from the UK to South America, sailing outward via Lisbon and Las Palmas, to Rio de Janeiro, Santos, Montevideo and finally Buenos Aires. They returned with chilled meat accommodated in six refrigerated holds which featured tween decks with refrigerated lockers. The **Uruguay Star** is seen in the Royal Docks at London in May 1972 and had accommodation for 53 first class passengers. She was the third vessel in this series and was completed in May 1948 with a gross tonnage of 10,723. Her main machinery consisted of three Cammell Laird-built steam turbines developing 8,700shp and driving a single propeller shaft via double reduction gearing. Two oil-fired Babcock and Wilcox water-tube boilers provided the steam required and a normal service speed of 16 knots was expected. The **Uruguay Star** was sold for breaking up at Kaohsiung arriving there in August 1972. However, one of her sisters, the **Paraguay Star** had a less fortunate end. She caught fire whilst berthed in the Royal Victoria Docks in London on 12 August 1969, and was subsequently sold for breaking up at Hamburg later that year.

(the late C C Beazley)

Vessels of the Port Line Ltd were frequent visitors to Cardiff with refrigerated produce from New Zealand, and here we have a fine example, the **Port Nicholson**. She is seen sailing from the port on 20 June 1974 having discharged her cargo of meat and dairy produce. She was a fast twin-screw motor cargo liner completed in November 1962 by Harland & Wolff's shipyard at Belfast. At 14,972grt she was the largest ship in the Port Line fleet when delivered and had six holds with a total refrigerated capacity of 603,810 cubic feet. The **Port Nicholson** was designed for the New Zealand trade and had accommodation for twelve passengers, while her officers and crew enjoyed good facilities including a hobbies room. She had a pair of 6-cylinder Burmeister & Wain two-stroke diesels built by the shipyard, and designed to be run on heavy fuel oil. They gave the **Port Nicholson** a service speed of 18$\frac{1}{4}$ knots, although on trials she came close to 21 knots. An interesting feature for the period was the installation of an AC electrical system, later to become commonplace on ships by the 1970s. The **Port Nicholson** was another victim of containerisation and by the late 1970s was obsolete in many respects. After giving her owner just seventeen years' service, she was sold in October 1979, and the following month arrived at Kaohsiung in Taiwan for breaking up, a sad end to an elegant ship.

(John Wiltshire)

Axel Johnson and others founded the shipping company AB Nordstjernan on 19 May 1890. In 1904 the Johnson Line name was introduced to coincide with a new service to South America, and by 1914 there were also routes to the North Pacific and North American West coast. The *Bolivia* was an elegant cargo liner completed in September 1946. She was one of a series of similar vessels built for Johnson Line in the 1940s which included the *Brasil*, *Guayana* and *Panama*. They were derived from a late 1920s three-island design, hence the counter-stern. The *Bolivia* was built in Gothenburg by A/B Götaverken with a gross tonnage of 7,133 and an overall length of 455 feet, and could provide accommodation for twenty-four passengers. She had some refrigerated capacity and was a twin-screw motorship powered by a pair of A/B Götaverken diesels. In 1971 she passed to Ybarra Compania SA of Spain as *Balboa*, nominally owned in Panama by Compania Naviera Americana de Vapores SA. What a magnificent sight she makes when viewed from the Erskine Bridge on the Clyde on 5 July 1978, bound for Glasgow. She had previously loaded at Liverpool, having been chartered in the UK for the west coast BHLR (Blue Star, Houlder, Lamport & Holt, Royal Mail) conference service to South America. Sold at Barcelona in September 1978, the *Balboa* soon sailed for Karachi as *Shaheen I*, retaining her Panamanian registry. She later arrived at Gadani Beach on 11 February 1979 for breaking up.

(Paul Boot)

The **Maryland** was one of a class of four cargo liners with unusual split superstructure, trunked hatch and the machinery space situated three-quarters aft. They were completed in France for Compagnie Générale Transatlantique (CGT) between 1958 and 1960. The lead vessel was the **Magellan** which was initially allocated to CGT's South Pacific service, but later joined her sisters **Maryland**, **Michigan** and **Mississippi** on the North Pacific run. The **Maryland** is seen arriving at Eastham on 24 February 1973 on a Euro-Pacific service from Canadian Pacific coast ports to Europe. This was jointly operated by French Line CGT, HAPAG and Holland-America Line. She dated from 1958 having being launched on 28 June that year at the yard of Chantiers et Ateliers de Provence, Port-de-Bouc, and was completed with a gross tonnage of 9,224 and an overall length of 490 feet. She featured a long forecastle and had five holds which included 15,091 cubic feet of refrigerated stowage. All the accommodation space was air-conditioned and there was provision for twelve passengers. All four ships in this class were fitted with a Doxford opposed-piston type diesel engine built by the shipyard, and developing 9,000bhp at 120rpm. They were ultimately superseded by container ships, and the **Maryland** and **Michigan** were sold in 1976 to Singapore Islands Line Pte Ltd, becoming **Senang Island** and **Brani Island** respectively. The **Senang Island** was sold for demolition at Gadani Beach in May 1981, while the **Brani Island** had met her end there the previous year.

(Paul Boot)

The Spanish shipping company Naviera Aznar SA (Aznar Line), formerly Sota y Aznar, had operated passenger services to South America, the Caribbean and the United States, and from 1952 introduced a service from the Canary Islands to London and later Liverpool. Two very smart passenger cargo liners, the **Monte Udala** and **Monte Urbasa** entered the fleet in 1948, and were joined in 1952 by the **Monte Ulia**. She was a much more modern looking ship and had been launched at Bilbao by Sociedad Española de Construccion Naval, as **Monasterio de El Escorial** for Empresa Nacional "Elcano" SA. She had a gross tonnage of 10,123 with an overall length of 487 feet, and accommodation for 114 passengers. The **Monte Ulia** was powered by a 10-cylinder Sulzer diesel engine of 7,300bhp giving her a speed of 16½ knots, and she was the largest vessel in the fleet at that time. Aznar Line began operating cruises during the 1960s, and this may have been the service in which she was engaged as we see her sailing from Southampton in the autumn of 1972. However, the **Monte Ulia** was sold in 1976, passing to Climax Shipping Corporation, a division of Maldives Shipping, as **Climax Opal** registered in Singapore. Her future was cut short following a serious accommodation fire while at Belfast on 2 April 1977. She was declared a constructive total loss and was subsequently delivered to Spanish shipbreakers at Santander in June 1977. Aznar Line ceased to trade in 1983.

(Bernard McCall collection)

CLYDE-BUILT We now see a selection of vessels that were products of the Clyde's once thriving shipyards. Three cargo liners were ordered in 1961 from Greenock Dockyard Ltd on the Clyde, and were a development of the *Clan Fergusson* type. It was intended that the three new ships would receive King Line names with *King Canute* being allocated to the initial vessel. There was a change in policy and the ship was launched on 22 May 1962 bearing the name *Clan Macgillivray* and completed in late August for King Line Ltd with Cayzer, Irvine & Co Ltd as her managers. Her two sisters, *Clan Macgregor* and *Clan Macgowan* followed in December 1962 and April 1963. Ownership soon transferred to The Clan Line Steamers Ltd, London but this would change again later on. The *Clan*

Macgillivray was heralded as the first British ship to have a substantial element of automation in her engine room, which featured an air-conditioned control room and much remote control of her machinery and auxiliaries. She featured improved accommodation and her five holds were fitted with steel hatch covers throughout. Her holds were designed to allow the use of forklift trucks and her No 1 lower tween deck could carry 150 tons of dangerous cargo. The *Clan Macgillivray* had a speed of $16^{1/2}$ knots and she is seen arriving at Avonmouth on 23 March 1972. She was sold to Anglo-Eastern Shipping Co Ltd of Hong Kong in 1981 becoming *Clan Macboyd*, and was broken up at Shanghai in 1984.

(John Wiltshire)

The post-war rebuilding programme for P&O Group subsidiaries Federal Steam Navigation Co Ltd and New Zealand Shipping Co Ltd commenced with the delivery in 1947 of the **Norfolk** and **Haparangi**, the first of eight *H-class* refrigerated cargo liners. The **Cumberland**, **Hertford**, **Huntingdon** and **Hurunui** all appeared in 1948, while the **Sussex** and **Hinakura** were completed in 1949. These were large twin-screw ships, capable of carrying in the region of 522,000 cubic feet of refrigerated produce and had six holds. The **Norfolk** was delivered to Federal Steam Navigation Co Ltd, but in 1953 became **Hauraki** for New Zealand Shipping Co Ltd. She was built by John Brown & Co Ltd of Clydebank and had a gross tonnage of 11,272. Her main engines were a pair of 5-cylinder Doxford-type diesels built by John Brown and developing 12,800bhp. In 1966 the **Hauraki** came under the ownership of Federal Steam Navigation Co Ltd, and with New Zealand Shipping Co Ltd as her managers. This is how we see her whilst discharging at Cardiff on 6 March 1970. In October 1971 her managers became P&O General Cargo Division, and from April 1973 her owners were Peninsular & Oriental Steam Navigation Company, London. Her useful days were at an end, thanks to the growing move to containerisation, and the **Hauraki** was delivered to breakers at Kaohsiung on Christmas Day 1973.

(John Wiltshire)

In 1924, the shipping agents Birt, Potter and Hughes (who were behind the formation of the Federal Steam Navigation Company in the mid-1890s) established the Avenue Shipping Co as their shipowning division. Although wound up in 1934, Avenue Shipping Co Ltd was revived in September 1954 as a result of the desire to separate the non-refrigerated ships within New Zealand Shipping, and make them available to other P&O Group companies. Managed by Trinder Anderson & Co Ltd, the initial fleet in 1954/55 consisted of five pre-war former New Zealand Shipping vessels. Meanwhile in 1952, a new vessel named **Enton** was placed into the ownership of Birt, Potter and Hughes. In 1955 this was transferred to the fleet as the **Limerick**, and then a new building programme began. This saw the delivery of the **Donegal** in 1957, **Galway** in 1959 and finally the **Antrim**. The **Antrim** was launched 19 January 1962 at the yard of A Stephen & Sons Ltd, Linthouse, on the Clyde near Glasgow. By 1971 just three ships remained in the Avenue fleet, and management of these duly passed to P&O General Cargo Division in that October, with ownership changing to P&O in May 1972. As can be seen, the **Antrim** has retained her name and livery when photographed arriving at Tilbury in the autumn of 1974, but early in 1975 she was renamed **Strathinch**. She was sold in late 1977 to Highwater Navigation Co Ltd, of Chittagong, and renamed **Islami Taaj** under the Bangladeshi flag. As the Hong Kong-owned **Singapore 2**, she stranded on the west coast of South Korea on 16 July 1982, and was broken up at Inchon soon afterwards.

(Douglas Cromby collection)

The **Loosdrecht** was launched on 16 May 1950 and completed in September as **Langleeclyde** for Medomsley Steam Shipping Co Ltd of London, a subsidiary of Phs Van Ommeren NV of Rotterdam. She was a 15-knot vessel of 6,557grt completed by Blythswood Shipbuilding Co Ltd at Scotstoun in Glasgow, and had an overall length of 487 feet. She had accommodation for twelve passengers, tunnel side tanks for the carriage of vegetable oils and her cargo handling gear included a 50 ton derrick. She was transferred to the Dutch flag in 1961 as the **Loosdrecht** under the nominal ownership of NV Stoomvaart Mij "De Maas". She was an interesting visitor to Cardiff when photographed on the Empire Wharf on 16 May 1968, and carrying the distinctive funnel colours of United Netherlands Steamship Company. The **Loosdrecht** became **Spalmatori Seaman** in 1968 when she was sold to Marvigia Compania Naviera SA, and flew the Greek flag registered in Piraeus. From 1975 she could be found sailing as the Panamanian-flagged **Wan Fu** for Wan Fu Steamship Company SA, and following collision damage sustained in November 1977 was sent for scrap in Taiwan, arriving at the Kaohsiung yard of Chu Feng Industrial Co Ltd on 28 June 1978.

(John Wiltshire)

In 1949 the shipbuilder Greenock Dockyard Co Ltd had a number of steam turbine-powered cargo liners on its order books for Clan Line Steamers Ltd. The first pair emerged in 1950 as **Clan Shaw** and **Clan Sinclair**, but the next pair intended to be **Clan Skene** and **Clan Stewart** were not delivered, and the vessels were completed for Pacific Steam Navigation Co as **Kenuta** and **Flamenco** in 1950. Their new owner was obviously satisfied with this new tonnage as a further two similar vessels were ordered from Greenock Dockyard, and a third from Wm Denny at Dumbarton. This trio took the names **Potosi**, **Pizarro** and **Cotopaxi**, and were employed on PSNC's traditional South American cargo services. The **Potosi** is named after a city in Bolivia and is noted here at Swansea on 5 September 1972. She had been completed in May 1955 and had a gross tonnage of 8,564, while her power plant consisted of three Parsons steam turbines developing 10,340shp, with steam supplied by a pair of oil-fired water-tube boilers. The **Flamenco** had been sold by 1966, but the remaining four continued to sail until the early 1970s. The **Potosi** was sold in 1972 to Greek owner Gourdomichalis Maritime SA and became **Kavo Peiratis**. She returned to the Clyde to be scrapped at Dalmuir in late 1976.

(John Wiltshire)

On 10 March 1972 the **North Countess** was a visitor to the repair jetty in Swansea's Queen's Dock when she was caught on film on what can only be described as a glorious day. She was built as **North Countess** by Blythswood Shipbuilding Co Ltd at Glasgow as their yard number 123, and was completed in August 1958. She was built for A G Pappadakis, a London-based Greek shipowner who also took a similar ship, the **North Empress**, in 1957. The **North Countess** was registered to Panconquista Compania Naviera SA under the Liberian flag, but switched to Greek registry in 1961. She was a closed shelter deck type freighter with a gross tonnage of 10,662 and an overall length of 531 feet. Her main engine was of the type found in many tramp ships of this period, an opposed-piston Doxford. In this case it was a 6-cylinder version built by Hawthorn, Leslie (Eng) Ltd, developing 7,200bhp and giving the **North Countess** a speed of 15 knots. She was sold in 1979 to become **Athina** for Martlet Maritime Inc (D Apessakis), of Piraeus, and from 9 November 1981 went into lay-up at nearby Eleusis. It is reported that, in 1984, she was renamed **Titi** by her owner but then sold to SBI Enterprises Ltd, sailing as **Span** under the Maltese flag for the voyage to Gadani Beach for breaking, where she was beached on 20 March 1984.

(John Wiltshire)

SOME TYPICAL TRAMP SHIPS Queen Alexandra Dock at Cardiff is the location for this fine view of the Greek tramp ship *Irini*, taken in the late afternoon sunshine of 12 September 1973 towards the end of a charter to Elder Dempster Line. The *Irini* was the former British freighter *Temple Main*, and the final example of a trio of tramp ships built in Scottish shipyards for Temple Steamship Co Ltd of London, and managed by Lambert Bros (Shipping) Ltd. The first two ships were completed in 1954 as *Temple Hall* and *Temple Lane*, with the latter being a product of Lithgows Ltd at Port Glasgow. The third ship, the *Temple Main* was completed in April 1958, and like the *Temple Hall* was built by Caledon Shipbuilding and Engineering Co Ltd at Dundee. She had a gross tonnage of 8,005 and an overall length of 458 feet. She was of five-hatch layout, although there were only four cargo holds. Her masts, as can be seen here, are of the distinctive bipod design, while her derricks included one of 30-ton capacity. All three ships in the series had the popular 4-cylinder Doxford-type opposed-piston diesel, and in this vessel it was built under licence by D Rowan & Co Ltd. The *Temple Main* became *Irini* in 1969 for Syros Shipping Co (L M Valmas and Son) of Piraeus. She was laid up at Stylis from 24 June 1982 and made her last voyage to breakers at Gadani Beach during the summer of 1984 as *Spirit* under the Maltese flag.

(John Wiltshire)

Bank Line Ltd (Andrew Weir and Co Ltd) embarked on a fleet renewal programme in the early 1950s with the aim of maintaining a fleet of around fifty tweendeck general cargo ships. Harland and Wolff delivered six vessels in the years 1953 to 1955, before a much larger order was placed for thirty-eight ships for delivery between 1957 and 1964. These were 12,000dwt vessels, and construction was split between Harland and Wolff at Belfast and Wm Doxford at Sunderland. Doxford completed twenty-one of these commencing with the **Firbank** in 1957. As deliveries gathered pace there were numerous detailed changes to the design. The **Forresbank** was delivered in 1962 and was a near sister to the **Trentbank**. Both featured a raised poop deck, twin king posts forward and a tapered funnel with a rounded top. The **Forresbank** had an overall length of 487 feet and a gross tonnage of 8,587 when operating as a closed shelter deck ship. She had five holds and six deep tanks for vegetable oils, and was powered by a 4-cylinder Doxford P-type engine of 6,640bhp. In 1978 the **Forresbank** was sold to Cypriot-flag Hartford Navigation Company (S C Vazeos of Piraeus) as **Veesky**, and is seen as such at Singapore Western Anchorage on 18 June 1980. She was broken up as **Admiral** at Alang in 1983. The similar former **Willowbank** of 1960, sailed as **Veestar** for Kea Shipping Co Ltd, Limassol (also S C Vazeos) from 1978 until 1982.

(Nigel Jones)

The Panamanian-flagged tramp ship **Armadora** is seen manoeuvring in Queen Alexandra Dock at Cardiff on 14 November 1971, having just arrived to load a cargo for Bombay. She sailed two days later calling at Las Palmas on 24 November, on what was probably her last loaded voyage. Her owner went on to rename her **Viva X** in early 1972. This marked the end of her thirty-three year career as she was immediately sold to Chou's Iron Works at Kaohsiung, Taiwan, in February that year for breaking up. The **Armadora** was owned by Meridional Armadora SA, and had been launched way back on 10 October 1938 as **Anatina** for A/S Anatina (Marcus Chr Stray) of Kristiansand, Norway. She was completed by Öresundsvarvet A/B, Landskrona, with a gross tonnage of 4,986 and an overall length of 453 feet. She was a motorship with four British Polar-design 6-cylinder Atlas diesels with a total output of 4,400bhp. These provided transmission via electro-magnetic slip couplings and single reduction gearing to a single propeller. The vessel had a recorded speed of between 13 and 14 knots. In 1962 she became **Gardøy** for Einar M Gaard A/S of Haugesund, and in 1967 took the name **Ela**, while flying the flag of Israel for Ships Mediterranean Lines West Africa Ltd (Ofer Brothers) of Haifa.

(John Wiltshire)

In this photograph we can take a good look at the lines of the hull of the Scandinavian-built cargo ship **Tayeb**. She is moored at Britannia Quay in the Roath Basin at Cardiff on 26 June 1971, and could be under repair or perhaps waiting to go into drydock. She flies the flag of Dubai which was rarely seen in a South Wales port, and was owned by Dubai National Shipping Corporation. She was launched on 31 August 1948 by the Norwegian shipyard A/S Fredrikstad M/V at Fredrikstad, and completed in November that year as **Foldal** for A/S Moltzau's Tankrederi of Oslo. She was not a large ship and had a gross tonnage of just 2,385 and overall length of just 351 feet. She was a steamship and her machinery consisted of a

4-cylinder compound expansion engine of 3,000ihp built by the shipyard and featured an oil-fired boiler. Three other names were carried prior to becoming **Tayeb** in 1971. Perhaps her most significant period was from 1950 until 1963 as **Murcia** and sailing for Rederi A/B Svenska Lloyd (Swedish Lloyd) of Gothenburg, although she later spent six years with Finnish owners as **Espa**. Tragically the **Tayeb** was lost on 8 February 1972, when she dragged her anchor off Port Louis, Mauritius, and was wrecked on a reef with the loss of seven lives.

(John Wiltshire)

Sociedad Transoceanica Canopus SA was a Panama-based ship management company that had been operated by London Greek shipowners Rethymnis & Kulukundis since 1949. They took delivery of the Greek-registered tramp ship **Centaurus**, which had been completed in the Netherlands in March 1962 by J & K Smit's Scheepswerf at Kinderdijk. She was an attractive ship of 10,493 gross tons and was constructed as a closed shelterdeck vessel of three-quarters aft layout. The **Centaurus** had an overall length of 516 feet and she was powered by a 6-cylinder Stork diesel of 7,050bhp, which gave her a respectable speed of 16½ knots. In 1965 her owners became Co-Ventura Compania Naviera SA, but she remained with Rethymnis and Kulukundis, registered in Piraeus, and nominally managed by Sociedad Transoceanica Canopus SA. She is seen at Barry on 30 January 1972, having sailed from Mackay, Australia, on 10 November 1971, calling at Cape Town on 7 December, and having probably discharged at Avonmouth. In 1973 she was sold to Seama International Shipping Ltd (S M Anwar and V N Mavreas) of London, and registered in Famagusta as **Amber**. She was laid up at Karachi from July 1983 until 23 December 1984 when she was run ashore at nearby Gadani Beach for demolition.

(the late T W Wiltshire)

On the evening high tide of 14 July 1969 the steamship **Sonja** has just made her way down the River Avon from Bristol City Docks, and is heading into the Severn Estuary and the open sea beyond. The **Sonja** was completed in August 1940 for the account of her Swedish builder, Helsingborgs Varfs A/B at Helsingborg. Shortly after completion, she passed to A/B Transatlantic Marine (Transmarin) of Helsingborg. She was classed as an open shelterdeck ship with a gross tonnage of 1,569, and her hull was strengthened to operate in ice. The **Sonja** had four holds and was powered by a triple expansion engine with an output of 1,150ihp, which gave her a speed of 9¾ knots. Passing in August 1963 to the Stockholm-based Arved Magi, under the nominal ownership of Estoco Shipping Co Ltd, Monrovia, she was chartered back to Transmarin until laid up at Europoort in April 1975. Interestingly, she had been transferred to the Panamanian flag in November 1973 when the Liberian flag authorities no longer permitted ships over twenty years old on their register. In December 1975 she became the Panamanian-flagged **Captain Antonis** for North Sea and West Indies SA and continued trading until 1978. Following a call at London, she loaded a cargo of cement at Szczecin for Lagos. She was then laid up and abandoned at Abidjan in July that year, and after failing to track down her owners, was scuttled near that port on 31 July 1979.

(John Wiltshire)

The Greek-registered motorship *Irene* is seen underway off Woolwich in July 1969, and was a truly remarkable survivor. Her service speed was around 10 knots and her main engine, believed to be original, was a 1,600bhp four-stroke 6-cylinder diesel built by A/B Götaverken to a Burmeister and Wain design. It was on 21 March 1921 that she was launched as *Sulina* for AB Sweden-Levant (Broström), Gothenburg. She was constructed at the shipyard of Öresundsvarvet A/B at Landskrona and with a gross tonnage of 2,978 was delivered to her owners on 24 August. She had an overall length of 316 feet, and her hull was strengthened to operate in ice. In 1927 she became *Sparreholm* for AB Swedish American Line and in 1936 was sold to Bergen-based Stamers Rederi A/S as *Heimgar* under the Norwegian flag. After surviving WWII she passed to Finnish owner Finland Steamship Ltd (Finska) of Helsinki, who continued to sail her for sixteen years as *Hesperus*. In this 1969 view with the name *Irene* she is working for Stavros A Daifas of Piraeus who acquired her in 1963. Her days were numbered as she was about to meet a dramatic end. On 9 September 1969 she had been discharging phosphate at Selata, Lebanon. In order to seek shelter from a storm, her master made the decision to leave port and drop anchor. However, she was wrecked after running aground just outside the harbour and her crew had to be rescued.

(the late C C Beazley)

The Bowater Steamship Co Ltd was founded in 1955 and was soon operating three steam turbine-powered newsprint carriers on services from Newfoundland in Canada to the United Kingdom. Subsequently, six smaller new vessels were added to the fleet between 1958 and 1961. These were known as forest product carriers and were designed to carry newsprint and baled pulp on services from Baltic ports to the UK as well as from Newfoundland, and were built to navigate ice. The holds, fitted with MacGregor steel hatch covers, were constructed without any pillars or obstructions, and the ships could take up to 450 tons of deck cargo. The first of the six was completed at Dundee by Caledon Shipbuilding & Engineering Co Ltd as **Elizabeth Bowater**, followed closely by **Constance Bowater** in August 1958. Caledon built the final vessel in the series, **Nina Bowater**, in 1961, while two came from Wm Denny at Dumbarton and another from Cammell Laird at Birkenhead. This photograph shows the former **Constance Bowater** now sailing as the Piraeus-registered **Kretan Spirit**, having been sold by Bowaters in 1972. She is making her way up the Shatt-al-Arab waterway near Abadan on 18 May 1980. Her owner was listed as Maria Victoria Naviera SA, a company run by New York-based Greek shipowner Andreas Markakis who, in 1977, went on to purchase the **Nina Bowater**, naming her **Kretan Glory**. Laid up in a damaged condition at Acajutla, El Salvador, in June 1982, the **Kretan Spirit** was broken up at Cartagena in Colombia in 1985.

(Andrew Wiltshire)

A number of Greek shipowners took delivery of new tramp ships in the 1950s through to the early 1970s. Many of these were constructed in the shipyards of north-east England and one such example was the **Aghios Spyridon**. She was built for Syra-based shipowners Minas Rethymnis, Michael Pneumaticos and Stathis Yanaghas and her owners from new were described as Porto Blanco Compania Naviera SA. The **Aghios Spyridon** was completed by Wm Doxford & Sons (Shipbuilders) Ltd, Sunderland in July 1957 with a gross tonnage of 9,924 and overall length of 509 feet. She was of the traditional and by now obsolete split superstructure layout with five hatches and accommodation for ten passengers. The main engine was typically a Doxford, in this case a 6-cylinder variant developing 6,800bhp and giving the vessel a speed of 15 knots. In 1965 the title of her recorded owner was changed to Compañia de Navegacion Golfo Azul SA, but remained within the Rethymnis group. The **Aghios Spyridon** is seen off Montreal in the summer of 1968. In 1974 she passed to another Greek owner, Navarino Shipping and Transport (M P Tsikopoulos) as **Trinity**. She was eventually broken up at Inchon in South Korea during 1979.

(René Beauchamp)

The **Bordagain** is a very good example of a former British-owned purpose-built tramp ship, in this case enjoying a further lease of life under the Liberian flag. She was new in 1958 as **Baron Garioch** delivered by J Readhead & Sons Ltd, South Shields, to Kelvin Shipping Co Ltd and managed by H Hogarth and Sons Ltd. Hogarth had received six new tramp ships between 1954 and 1956 featuring triple expansion steam engines, enhanced by a low pressure turbine. The **Baron Garioch** was the second vessel in a new series of eight diesel-powered tramps which commenced in 1958 with the **Baron Jedburgh**, also from Readhead's yard. The **Baron Garioch** has the classic lines of a five-hold dry-cargo ship with split superstructure, and a gross tonnage of 8,337. She was fitted with a Doxford-type opposed-piston oil engine of 4,400bhp, built by Hawthorn Leslie (Eng) Ltd, and which was reputed to burn between $13\frac{1}{2}$ and 14 tons of diesel per day when running at 115rpm. She became **Bordagain** in 1968 upon sale to the Basque owner Ramón De La Sota Jr, and in this view is seen arriving at Swansea from Valparaiso on 28 June 1969. In 1976 she passed to Greek owners Costas V Paterasas as **Erini Patera**, registered in Piraeus, and was ultimately broken up at Bombay in the summer of 1982 after a period in lay up.

(John Wiltshire)

The West German-flagged **Nedderland** was a truly remarkable survivor, and a fine example of a very early motor cargo liner. She was one of a small group of vessels ordered by Swedish shipowner Axel Johnson from the yard of Burmeister & Wain at Copenhagen. As the **Pacific** she was completed in 1914, and in 1951 passed to German owner Hugo Stinnes after surviving WWII when, from April 1940, she was chartered to the British War Ministry. Renamed **Ellen Hugo Stinnes** in 1951, she was rebuilt and modernised in 1956. On 11 August 1961 she arrived at Bremen for repairs by Atlas-Werke AG who eventually bought the ship and, in 1963, re-engined her after her owners had met with financial difficulties. In May 1964 she was chartered to M Gehrckens of Hamburg and renamed **Steinweg**. By now her gross tonnage was given as 3,731 and her overall length was 380 feet. In 1966 she returned to Hugo Stinnes Transozean Schiffahrt GmbH and registered at Hamburg regained her earlier name **Ellen Hugo Stinnes**. This grand old lady was still plying the oceans when in 1971 she passed at auction to Friedrich Krupp GmbH and in 1973 to Carl Meentzen of Bremen and became **Nedderand**. This is how we see her on 7 September 1976, making her way along the New Waterway. In 1978, she passed to the Singapore-based flag of convenience owner, Ensenada Armadora SA, Panama, who renamed her **Castos**. Detained by the authorities at Calcutta in March 1979, she was broken up locally in late 1980.

(John Wiltshire collection)

GERMAN-BUILT CARGO SHIPS The *Tundraland* was the final vessel in a series of five cargo ships built for A/B Svenska Orient Linien (William Thorén) (Swedish Orient Line) of Gothenburg between 1955 and 1958. The other ships were the *Thuleland* and *Tavastland* of 1955, *Timmerland* of 1956 and *Traneland* of 1957. The *Tundraland* was completed in March 1958 by AG "Weser" at Bremen with a gross tonnage of 3,714 and an overall length of 393 feet. She was of five-hatch layout with some refrigerated space and was certified to carry eight passengers. Her hull was strengthened for navigation in ice on the St Lawrence Seaway, and she had a summer loaded draught of 21ft 4in. The *Tundraland* was powered by a 6-cylinder MAN diesel developing 3,950bhp and she had a service speed of 15 knots. By 1973 she was recorded as being owned by Resolute Shipping Ltd, a joint venture between Broström and Fednav, initially registered in Newcastle, where she berthed on 7 December, and later in Montreal. In this view the *Tundraland*, still in Broström colours, is seen arriving at Valletta in Malta in June 1978. Her Swedish Orient Line service soon ended and she became wholly owned by Fednav (Federal Commerce and Navigation). Her first change of name came in 1981 when she became *Arctic Tide* for Arctic Shipping Co Ltd of Halifax, Nova Scotia, but registered at Georgetown in Grand Cayman. Laid up for repairs at New York from October 1981 to June 1982, she was transferred to the Cardiff Transportation Co Ltd, for her final days which ended in September 1983 when she was broken up at Gadani Beach.

(Alastair Paterson)

The Hamburg South America Line (Hamburg-Sudamerikanische DG Eggert u Amsinck) was founded in 1871 and commenced operating passenger services to Rio de Janeiro, Santos and the River Plate. Following WWII, services were not permitted to resume until 1951 and a fleet renewal took place. A number of motorships were delivered from the Hamburg yard of Howaldtswerke AG-Werk, and two of these stood out from the others. They were the **Santa Teresa** and **Santa Inés**, both delivered in early 1953, and were modern stylish passenger cargo liners, for deployment on the service to Brazil, Uruguay and Argentina. They featured luxurious passenger accommodation, with all cabins being outboard with private bathrooms and air conditioning. The two sisters had five cargo holds, at least two of which were refrigerated for the carriage of meat and other perishables, while there were also heated tanks for vegetable oils. The expansion of air travel had made its mark by 1960 and Hamburg South America Line decided to concentrate on cargo vessels. Both ships were sold in 1961 with the **Santa Inés** passing to Trans-Oceanic SS Co Ltd, Karachi, as **Ocean Energy**. Having discharged crushed bones in Roath Dock at Cardiff, we now find her loading scrap metal in Roath Basin on 11 June 1974. In this year Pakistan's shipping industry was nationalised and her owner became the Pakistan Shipping Corporation, and from 1978 the Pakistan National Shipping Corporation. She ended her days with shipbreakers at Gadani Beach in 1980.

(John Wiltshire)

The Cypriot-flagged motor cargo ship **Lass** is seen arriving at Fraserburgh in early 1975 to load cargo for Chioggia, Italy. She was launched as **Heluan** by Deutsche Werft AG at Hamburg on 16 May 1951 and completed by the end of July. As **Heluan** she was delivered to Ernst Komrowski Reederei, Hamburg, a company founded in 1923 and still trading in 2014 with three container ships and a bulk carrier. She had a gross tonnage of 1,544 and a deadweight of 2,400, and featured a low bridge house and collapsible masts. Her hull has a distinctive raised quarterdeck layout and at 270 feet overall length comprised two cargo holds served by two hatches. Her speed was quoted as 11 knots and she was powered by a 6-cylinder Motorenwerke Mannheim (MWM) diesel developing 1,000bhp, which it is thought was fitted in 1961. The **Heluan** was flagged out to Cyprus in 1971 and renamed **Lass** in 1972 under the beneficial ownership of A Tangos of Piraeus. On 17 October 1979 a fire broke out on board the **Lass** while she was on passage from Italy to Beirut, in the Mediterranean south of Greece, with a cargo of steel bars. She was subsequently towed to Greece and broken up at Perama during April 1980.

(Alastair Paterson)

The Pakistan Shipping Corporation operated a fleet of approximately twenty-seven ocean-going vessels in 1971. Of these just three were steam- powered and seven were known to be of British origin. These included the unusual **Karotua** and **Swat**, being the former Watts, Watts motorships **Weybridge** and **Wimbledon** of 1958. There were eleven new builds between 1965 and 1969, some of which could be described as attractive cargo vessels, while others were distinctive but no doubt functional. A very recently acquired but elderly member of the Pakistan fleet at this time was the German-built **Malam Jabba**, seen in Canadian waters at Varennes on the St Lawrence River in January 1971. She continued to trade for the National Shipping Corporation until 1977 when she passed to breakers at Gadani Beach in August that year. The **Malam Jabba** was completed in 1954 as **Welheim** for Kohlen-Import u Poseidon Schiffahrt AG of Hamburg. She was constructed by Lübecker Flender-Werke at Lübeck-Siems as an open shelterdeck/closed shelterdeck freighter with an overall length of 498 feet and a speed of 16 knots. She was a single-screw ship powered by a pair of 8-cylinder MAN diesels of 6,000bhp. In 1955 her owner changed to Kohlen-Import u Poseidon Schiffahrt AG, also of Hamburg, who went on to rename her **Transgermania** in 1963. She eventually became **Malam Jabba** in 1971.

(Marc Piché)

A number of Norddeutscher Lloyd cargo ships visited Cardiff in the late 1960s with aluminium ingots destined for the Alcan plant at Rogerstone, near Newport. These vessels came from North America and often called at ports on the continent, either prior to, but sometimes after, discharging at Cardiff. The **Blankenstein** was completed in August 1956 by Bremer Vulkan at Vegesack near Bremen, and had a gross tonnage of 8,053 with accommodation for five passengers. She was of five-hatch layout and her derricks included one of 50-ton capacity plus twenty in the $^1/2$ to 10-ton range. The **Blankenstein** was powered by an 8-cylinder Bremer Vulkan diesel of 9,000bhp. Norddeutscher Lloyd merged with Hamburg America Line in September 1970, to form Hapag-Lloyd AG, in whose colours we see the **Blankenstein** on 28 June 1973. The containers as deck cargo are a sure sign of the times. Other frequent visitors to Cardiff in this series of West German ships were the **Brandenstein** of 1952, **Burgenstein** and **Buchenstein**, both of 1958 and the **Buntenstein** of 1960. Upon her sale in 1977, the **Blankenstein** passed to Pacific International Lines Pte Ltd, Singapore, as **Kota Bakti**, and was eventually broken up at Kaohsiung, having arrived at her final destination in April 1983.

(John Wiltshire)

IN ICE The **Jeff Davis** was a fast cargo liner that sailed under the United States flag for Waterman Steamship Corporation of Mobile, Alabama. She is seen in heavy ice proceeding upbound at Vechères on the St Lawrence River on 17 January 1981, when trading to Leningrad. Noteworthy are the dummy funnel on top of the wheelhouse and the unusual design of her derricks. The **Jeff Davis** was previously owned by Pacific Far East Line Inc of San Francisco, a fleet that was formed just after WWII and affectionately became known as the Golden Bear Line. In this fleet she started out as **China Bear**, her keel being laid down in January 1961 at the shipyard of Bethlehem Steel Co, San Francisco. However, she was not completed until 27 June 1962, and followed her sistership **Philippine Bear** into service. Both ships were utilised on PFEL's transpacific service incorporating many advanced features, and were generally regarded as very good sea vessels too. The **China Bear** had a gross tonnage of 12,799 and naturally she was steam turbine driven with an impressive service speed of 23 knots. She was renamed **Canada Bear** in 1974, and was sold the following year to Waterman Steamship along with **Philippine Bear** which became **Nathanael Greene**. Both ships passed to the United States Government in 1983 and were broken up at Valencia in Spain during 1986. Pacific Far East Line went out of business in the late 1970s, as they were unable to make a successful transition to container operations.

(Marc Piché)

The *Egton* was a typical British-built tramp ship of the 1960s, but had rather mixed fortunes during her career which was spent entirely under British registry. She was completed in July 1962 for owners Rowland & Marwood's SS Co Ltd and registered at Whitby with Headlam & Son being her managers. She was of open shelter deck/closed shelter deck configuration, 507 feet overall length and constructed at the yard of Bartram & Sons Ltd, Sunderland. The *Egton* was powered by a 4-cylinder Doxford 670P4 oil engine of 6640bhp which gave her a speed of 14 knots. She joined the Headlam fleet which at that time consisted of two steamships and two motor vessels including the *Runswick* of 1956. The *Egton* was immediately laid up, and it was not until September 1963 that she undertook her maiden voyage which took her to Baie-Comeau to load grain for Liverpool. She was in trouble in January 1967 when she ran aground in Robin Hood's Bay and sustained serious bottom plate damage. To make matters worse, whilst being repaired on the Tyne she suffered a fire on board. The *Egton* returned to service in July 1967, and by 1972 was the only vessel in the Headlam fleet, but went into long-term lay up at Hartlepool in April 1977. She stayed until January 1986, by which time she was one of the last traditional pre-SD14 tramp ships under the Red Ensign. At this point her owners Headlam sold her to shipbreakers at Naantali in Finland, where she is seen arriving on 18 January 1986.

(K Brzoza)

Towards the very end of her active trading days the Soviet freighter *Stanislavskiy* is caught on camera on 17 January 1981, underway in heavy ice upbound on the St Lawrence River, off Ste Anne-de-Sorel and following a two-week ice jam. She had been completed nearly twenty-five years earlier at the Belgian shipyard of Jos Boel & Fils SA at Tamise. She was constructed as an open shelter deck vessel of 3,385 tons gross, with an overall length of 395 feet and breadth of 55 feet. Her main engine was a 6-cylinder Sulzer of 4,200bhp which gave her a speed of 14 knots. The *Stanislavskiy* was the first ship in a series of five from this yard, the other vessels being the *Nemirovich Danchenko*, *Vasiliy Kachalov*, *Leonid Leonidov* in 1957 and finally the *Ivan Moskvin* in 1958. The *Stanislavskiy* was originally registered in Leningrad but in later years was apparently sailing for the USSR (Murmansk Shipping Co) and registered in Murmansk. She was sold for scrap to a shipbreaker at La Arena in northern Spain in 1982, and a similar fate met three others of this class between 1981 and 1983. However, the *Leonid Leonidov* was recorded as surviving much longer; since 1991 being privately operated by Sevrybkholodflot of Murmansk. She finally arrived at Calcutta to be dismantled in 1995.

(Marc Piché)

Without doubt the SD14 was a very successful standard design, but the slightly larger SD15 offered by Austin & Pickersgill resulted in just one example, the **Armadale** of 1970. Brazilian shipbuilder, Companhia Comércio e Navegação (CCN), already licensed to build the SD14, eventually expressed an interest in the SD15 design. Between 1973 and 1988 they completed forty-three SD14s, and redeveloped the SD15 for the Brazilian market. Designated the PRINASA-121, it allowed for the carriage of containers and included a heavy-lift Stülcken derrick, and the installation of the locally-built Mecapesa MAN 11,550bhp 7-cylinder main engine. The first example was completed as **Amalia** in 1975 and a total of thirteen PRINASA-121s were constructed, all for Brazilian customers. The **Joana** was the third example and was launched on 5 May 1975 and completed over a year later in August 1976 for Companhia de Navegação Maritima Netumar. She had a gross tonnage of 10,297 and a speed of 17 knots. The **Joana** was 525 feet long with five holds, and her Stülcken derrick had a capacity of 60 tons. She was constructed to sail in ice and this is being put to the test on 22 March 1985 as she passes Vechères on the St Lawrence River outbound for Cabedello, Brazil. In 1989 she was sold and became **Sunderland Craftsman** for Vendome Marine Co Ltd, Cyprus (Blue Flag Navigation, Piraeus). Finally, in 1994, she was renamed **Panglima** for Rectagi Private Ltd (Jaya-JK Shipping) under Singapore registry. She was broken up in India at Alang during 2000.

(Marc Piché)

FAR EASTERN VARIETY The *Fides Progress* is very much a typical Japanese-built freighter completed in the 1950s, with her four sturdy goalpost masts. Her owner was Producer Corporation SA (Chip Seng Co Pte Ltd) and she was tramping under the Singapore flag. The *Fides Progress* is seen lying at anchor in Singapore Roads on 5 July 1977 and very much in need of cosmetic attention to her hull. She was launched on 30 December 1959 and completed in March 1960 as *Bolivia Maru* for Japanese owner Kawasaki Kisen KK, Kobe. She was a near sister to Kawasaki Kisen's *Peru Maru* of 1957, which was completed by the Kawasaki yard at Kobe. The *Bolivia Maru* was, however, constructed at the yard of Osaka Zosensho at Osaka, and with a gross tonnage of 8,174, had an overall length of 469 feet. Of closed shelter deck layout, the *Bolivia Maru* had six hatches and some refrigerated capacity within her holds. Her sixteen derricks ranged in size from 5-tons to 25-tons safe working load. Her main engine was a 6-cylinder Kawasaki Dockyard Company-built MAN design diesel of 5,600bhp, which gave her a speed of 14 knots. The *Fides Progress* was eventually broken up at Gadani Beach arriving there in January 1981.

(Douglas Cromby collection)

The China Ocean Shipping Company (COSCO) obtained many fine vessels that originated from the shipping fleets of northern Europe. Two such examples were the small general cargo ships **Lei Shan** and **Xiang Shan**, both dating from 1957. They were built in Germany by Bremer Vulkan, Vegesack, as **Spreestein** and **Siegstein** respectively for Norddeutscher Lloyd of Bremen. They were 413 feet in length, had five holds and were powered by a 6-cylinder Bremer Vulkan diesel. They passed to the newly-created Hapag-Lloyd fleet in 1970, and both were sold in 1972 to Nanyang Shipping Co of Mogadiscio (a front company for China managed by Ocean Tramping Co Ltd of Hong Kong) as **Minhao** and **Minai** under the Somali flag. In 1976 they passed to COSCO with whom they traded for five years. In this view we see the **Xiang Shan** at anchor in a pleasant setting at Port Klang, Malaysia, on 24 June 1980. Remarkably remaining as a pair, both the **Lei Shan** and **Xiang Shan** were sold to Sun-Line Limited of Hong Kong in 1981, and renamed **Ocean Jupiter** and **Ocean Mercury** respectively. Indicating continued mainland Chinese beneficial ownership, the **Ocean Jupiter** returned to COSCO ownership in 1983 as **Wan Ping**. However, the subject of our image, by now trading as **Ocean Mercury**, lasted until 1986 when she was sold to breakers at Kaohsiung. The **Wan Ping** on the other hand was transferred in 1987 to the Wuhu-based Anhui Ocean Shipping Company but eventually deleted from records.

(Nigel Jones)

The history of Kawasaki Kisen KK (K Line) can be traced back to 1919, and by the mid-1960s it controlled just over one hundred ships. As part of a fleet renewal programme, the **Holland Maru** was the second ship in a class of five fast cargo liners that Kawasaki Kisen was introducing on its Japan to northern Europe (via Suez Canal) route from 1965. The lead ship was the **Denmark Maru** and the **Holland Maru** was followed in 1966 by the **Sweden Maru**, **Norway Maru** and **Belgium Maru**. All were products of the Kawasaki Dockyard Co Ltd at Kobe, and the **Holland Maru** was completed in December 1965 with a grt of 8,866 and overall length of 496 feet. She had five holds and within these had a refrigerated capacity of 72,395 cubic feet. Her main engine was an MAN-type that developed 10,000bhp and gave a normal service speed of 17½ knots. In this view we see the **Holland Maru** at San Francisco in June 1968. An improved variant of this class was introduced in 1967 and comprised four vessels including the **Italy Maru** and **Portugal Maru**. The **Holland Maru** was sold in 1978 and became the Panamanian-flagged **Aquamarine** for Seiwa Kaiun KK of Tokyo and finally passed to the Government of Vietnam's Vietnam Sea Transport & Chartering Co, Saigon, early in 1986 as **Tra Bong**. After being idle at Saigon (Ho Chi Minh City) for much of 1987, she was broken up in Thailand.

(John Wiltshire collection)

The Union of Burma Five Star Line Corporation was established in 1959 as the state controlled deep-sea shipping fleet for Burma, and registered in Rangoon. The country was ruled by a military government from 1962 until 2011, and in 1990 many British derived names were changed. This resulted in Burma becoming known as Myanmar and its principal port Rangoon changed identity to Yangon. The shipping line was simply restyled Myanmar Five Star Line, Yangon. In 1963 Burma Five Star Line took delivery of four similar sized general cargo ships. These were *Ava* and *Bassein* from the German yard of AG "Weser" Werk Seebeck at Bremerhaven; and *Mergui* and *Pinya* from the Japanese yards of Uraga Dock and Hitachi Zosen respectively. The *Mergui* had a gross tonnage of 7,458, and was powered by a 5-cylinder Sulzer-type diesel of 5,500bhp, built by Uraga Dock and providing the *Mergui* with a service speed of 15½ knots. All four ships in this series visited northern Europe over the years and had very long trading careers, *Mergui* surviving a fire at Avonmouth in May 1973. In this view we see the *Mergui* lying in Singapore Roads on 12 June 2001, the enormous Stülcken derrick spoiling her otherwise attractive profile. She was renamed *Myeik* in 2002 by her owner, and was broken up in Myanmar late 2003. Her sister *Ava*, by now renamed *Inwa*, survived until May 2005.

(Douglas Cromby)

The Malaysian International Shipping Corporation (MISC) was founded in 1968, and based in Penang became the major shipping fleet for Malaysia. The **Bunga Melati** was one of a class of four similar cargo liners delivered to this fleet in 1971/72, from the Japanese shipyard of Mitsubishi Heavy Industries Ltd at Shimonoseki. The other ships were the **Bunga Orkid**, **Bunga Tanjong** and **Bunga Seroja**. Prior to this, in 1970, MISC had taken delivery of two longer six-hold ships the **Bunga Raya** and **Bunga Melor** from another shipyard in Japan. The **Bunga Melati** was completed in April 1972 with a gross tonnage of 10,702 and had five holds plus deep tanks for vegetable oils and latex. She featured a 60-ton heavy lift derrick as well as two 12½-ton electric cranes. The **Bunga Melati** is seen arriving at Cardiff from the Far East on 9 April 1975, when these ships were regular callers at the port to discharge. They then departed for the Thames to discharge vegetable oils or latex at Dagenham, before proceeding to the Royal Docks to load general cargo for the Far East. This often included old commercial vehicles for export. In 1982/83 the **Bunga Raya**, **Bunga Melor**, **Bunga Seroja** and **Bunga Melati** were converted into permanent containerships with fixed guides and the first two mentioned were also lengthened in the process. As a 574TEU containership, the **Bunga Melati** was sold in 1995 to Balaji Shipping Co SA under the Panamanian flag, managed by Seabridge SA of Lugano, as **Orient Spirit**, and was finally broken up at Alang in India in 1999.

(John Wiltshire)

FROM THE YARDS OF NORTH-EAST ENGLAND Charles Hill and Sons of Bristol established The Bristol City Line in 1879, and soon began operating services across the Atlantic. By 1933 there were regular services to New York and Canada, which in 1958 were extended to serve the Great Lakes. All their ships had names ending in *City*, and the 14-knot cargo ship **Bristol City** of 1959, was the fifth ship in the fleet to carry that name. She is seen arriving at Cardiff on 17 August 1969. Her recorded owner was Bristol City Line of Steamships Ltd, Bristol, with Charles Hill & Sons as her managers. She had an open shelter deck gross tonnage of 5,887, and was launched on 23 April 1959 by J Readhead & Sons Ltd at South Shields as yard number 600. The **Bristol City** was a steamship, the very last example for her owner. Her main machinery consisted of two Parsons Marine

steam turbines of 4500shp, and steam was supplied from a pair of oil-fired water-tube boilers. She was built with accommodation for five passengers and had an overall length of 459 feet. She was of five-hold layout, with six hatches and was provided with tunnel side tanks for the carriage of vegetable oils. The **Bristol City** was sold and handed over to Greek owners at Avonmouth in August 1970, becoming **Agelos Gabriel** for Gemini Compania Naviera SA (Christos Lemos), Piraeus. As such she was broken up in Yugoslavia by Brodospas at Split in April 1980 after nearly three years laid up at Chalkis. Bibby Line took full control of Bristol City Line in February 1972, after having bought into the company the previous year.

(John Wiltshire)

The **Al Murtaza** is a British-built tramp ship that is seen sailing here from Cardiff on 26 June 1976 having discharged a cargo of crushed bones. Although reported to have been transferred from private Pakistani to public ownership in 1974, it is thought she retained the colours of Muhammadi Steamship Co Ltd until she transferred to the Pakistan National Shipping Corporation in early 1979. She was completed in September 1955 by the Furness Shipbuilding Co Ltd at Haverton Hill on Teesside as **President Kruger**, and delivered to Northern Steamships Ltd, Cape Town. She had a gross tonnage of 8,299 and was powered by a 4-cylinder Hawthorn Leslie diesel of 4,400bhp, most probably of a Doxford design, giving the ship a speed of 13 knots. The clear poop deck and the three small goalpost masts should be noted. In 1959 she was sold to German owner "Union" Kabellegungs-u Schiffahrts-GmbH of Nordenham who renamed her **Neptun**. The intention was to convert her into a cable ship, but the scheme was abandoned and she was sold to Muhammadi Steamship Co Ltd in 1960 as **Al Murtaza**. She was finally operated by the Pakistan National Shipping Corporation from 1979, her final year of trading. She was broken up at Gadani Beach by Kohinoor Traders Ltd during 1980.

(John Wiltshire)

William McAndrew from Elgin, Scotland, had started trading in 1770 importing fruit to the UK from mainland Spain, Portugal and the Azores. In 1917 the family sold their business to the Royal Mail Group and MacAndrews & Co Ltd was formed in London. The revised spelling was intended to make pronunciation easier for the Spaniards. Subsequently acquired in 1935 by Andrew Weir and Company, a passenger and cargo service had commenced by 1938 from London to Gibraltar, Malaga, Cadiz and Seville. During WWII ten ships were lost to enemy action, but services to Lisbon, Gibraltar and Barcelona resumed in 1947. Two new cargo ships completed in August and October that year were the **Pinto** and **Pelayo**. Constructed at the Sunderland shipyard of William Doxford & Sons Ltd, they featured four holds for cargo, and were powered by 5-cylinder Doxford diesels of 4100bhp. The 2,576grt **Pinto** which was the second vessel for MacAndrews to carry this name, was sold to General Maritime Enterprises Corporation (Th A Papagelopoulos) in 1965, and was registered in Piraeus as **Panaghia P.**. She was a welcome visitor to Cardiff on 7 August 1970 laden with pit props from Archangel for the South Wales coalfield. The **Panaghia P.**, which also made a call at Barry in July 1973, survived until May 1978 when she was delivered to shipbreakers at Vigo, following a voyage to Lagos.

(John Wiltshire)

The Monarch Steamship Company Ltd was formed in 1902 and the fourth vessel to bear the name **British Monarch** joined the fleet in 1954. She is seen here moored on the Commissioner's Buoys at North Shields on 19 July 1962 and her pristine paintwork indicates that she has just come out of drydock. The **British Monarch** was launched on 12 September 1953 at the yard of Bartram & Sons Ltd, Sunderland, and completed with a gross tonnage of 5,806 and a length of 453 feet. The **British Monarch** was a typical tramp ship from one of the Sunderland shipyards at this time and was of open shelter deck layout. Seven bulkheads divided the ship into two holds and a deep tank forward, and two holds aft. Her main engine was a 7-cylinder Kincaid-built Burmeister & Wain of 2,600bhp resulting in a service speed of $11\frac{1}{4}$ knots. She was joined in 1959 by the larger tramp ship **Scottish Monarch**, and in 1960 Monarch Steamship was acquired by Harrisons (Clyde) Ltd and operated as a subsidiary. **British Monarch** was sold in 1964 to Mullion & Co Ltd of Hong Kong to become **Ardtara**. In 1967 the **Ardtara** was transferred to Mullion subsidiary Hyperion Shipping Co and renamed **Hyperion**, but shortly after this became **Rosetta Maud** for Redfern Shipping Co Ltd (Chris Moller) of London. The end came for the former **British Monarch** in 1972 when she was demolished at Gadani Beach.

(Malcolm Donnelly)

As part of a post-war rebuilding programme, Alfred Holt and Company introduced the first of the *A-class* motor vessels, the **Calchas**, to its Blue Funnel fleet in 1947. The *A-class* was similar in some ways to the earlier motorship **Priam** and comprised a series of twenty-six ships constructed over eleven years at four different shipyards. The **Ajax** was the last vessel in the series emerging in 1958, and was one of eleven *A-Class* from Vickers Armstrongs (Shipbuilders) Ltd at Newcastle. The **Ajax** was built at the High Walker shipyard, and delivered to China Mutual Steam Navigation Co Ltd (A Holt & Co) and registered at Liverpool. The **Ajax** with a gross tonnage of 7,969 was a three island cargo liner, with seven holds incorporating a small amount of refrigerated space. She was powered by a 6-cylinder Kincaid diesel of 8,000bhp, built under licence to a Burmester and Wain design. We see her sailing from Avonmouth on the afternoon tide of 21 May 1971. The following year, to release the name **Ajax** for a new bulk carrier, her owner renamed her **Deucalion** and in 1973 she was sold to Nan Yang Shipping Co, Mogadishu (a Chinese-owned company) as **Kailok** under the Somali flag. From 1976 she was sailing under the Panamanian flag for Brilliance Steamship Corporation SA (a new Chinese-owned subsidiary), retaining the name **Kailok**. In her twenty-fourth year this fine ship was despatched to shipbreakers at Kaohsiung arriving there in July 1982.

(John Wiltshire)

STARS AND STRIPES We shall now take a look at some steam-powered cargo ships sailing under the flag of the United States. American South African Lines (ASAL), a company owned by the Farrell family, took delivery of six impressive 16-knot cargo liners to standard design C3-S-BH2 in 1947. They were named *African Star*, *African Planet*, *African Rainbow*, *African Crescent*, *African Moon* and *African Lightning*. The first of the series was the *African Star* which was launched on 2 February 1946 by Federal Shipbuilding & Drydock Co, Kearny, and completed in April. With a gross tonnage of 7,972 she was an impressive ship with five holds, and her machinery consisted of a pair of 9,350shp General Electric Co steam turbines geared to a single propeller. ASAL became Farrell Lines in 1948,

and these ships were regularly employed on their cargo service from the US east coast to South African ports. Having been the mainstay on this service in the 1950s and early 1960s, they were eventually replaced by newer and bigger tonnage like the *African Comet* and *African Mercury*. Then from 1970 the older standard types began to reappear as back-up for the newer ships. As a result we have this glimpse of the *African Star* at Durban around Easter 1970. All six of the Farrell standard ships were sold in 1973 and subsequently delivered to shipbreakers at Kaohsiung that year. The *African Star* was renamed *Star* for owner American Condor Steamship Corporation, New York, and arrived at Kaohsiung on 3 December 1973 for breaking up.

(Trevor Jones)

The **Mormacscan** was one of eight cargo liners delivered to Moore-McCormack Lines Inc between 1960 and 1962 and included the **Mormacbay** and **Mormaccove**. The **Mormaccape** and **Mormacglen** were built by Todd Shipyards of San Pedro in California while the remainder were completed by Sun Shipbuilding and Drydock Company at Chester, Pennsylvania. The **Mormacscan** was completed in June 1961 and had a gross tonnage of 9,315. She was built with five holds and could also carry liquid cargoes in plastic- lined deep tanks. She had quick-operating hatch covers and a heavy lift derrick with a safe working load of 75 tons. Her accommodation with facilities for twelve passengers was made from a light alloy, and the funnel was actually a dummy, as two substantial exhaust uptakes located just aft performed this role. Her hull incorporated rubbing strakes and the ship was intended for Great Lakes Service. Main propulsion for the **Mormacscan** was by way of two General Electric Company steam turbines of 12,100shp, which gave her a speed of 19 knots. She is seen when still quite new at Montreal in this 1962 dated view. She became the **Scan** in 1977 coming under the control of the United States Government and was laid up in the National Defense Reserve Fleet on James River, Virginia. There she remained until her sale for breaking up at Brownsville, Texas, in 2007.

(the late Captain John Low [Marc Piché collection])

The **Louise Lykes** of 1965 was the first of a series of twelve ships that were constructed for Lykes Bros Steamship Company by Avondale Shipyards Inc at Avondale, near New Orleans. These modern cargo liners were to design C4-S-66a and were known as the *Gulf and Far East Clipper* class. They were designed to carry general and break-bulk cargoes from ports in the Gulf of Mexico to the Far East, including destinations such as Japan, Hong Kong, Korea, Taiwan and the Philippines. Typical cargoes included cotton, machinery, industrial chemicals as well as military cargoes like munitions. In this view taken from the then World Trade Centre in New Orleans, we see a brand new example of this class, the **Dolly Turman**, undertaking trials on the Mississippi in May 1967. Her gross tonnage was 10,723 and she had six cargo holds fitted with Wiley-Götaverken rotary hatch covers. Also visible is her cargo gear consisting of an 80-ton Stülcken derrick and twenty 15-ton derricks. Other innovative features include an 800hp bow thruster unit and an inorganic zinc rich coating on her superstructure to reduce maintenance. Her service speed was a smooth 20 knots, provided by a pair of De Laval steam turbines of 12,500shp. The **Dolly Turman** passed to the United States Government in 1986 to become part of their reserve fleet and was renamed **Cape Breton**. She has been laid up at Suisun Bay, north of San Francisco, since May 2012.

(Marc Piché collection)

The United States Lines Company of New York commissioned a fleet of ten fast cargo liners between June 1962 and October 1963. They featured six holds with ten hatches (three each on No 3 and No 4 holds) and had 26,710 cubic feet of refrigerated space. Cargo handling gear comprised twelve 10-ton and eight 15-ton derricks, plus a large 70-ton Stülcken heavy lift derrick. They also had wing ballast tanks along upper tween decks forward of the engine room, and flush decks to allow use of forklift trucks, and could carry over 1,000 tons of liquid cargoes in heated tanks. The ship in this view on the New Waterway on 9 April 1977 is the *Pioneer Commander*, which sailed as the *American Commander* until 1967. She was completed in April 1963 at the Fore River Shipyard of Bethlehem Steel at Quincy and had a gross tonnage of 11,185. Her main power plant consisted of two Bethlehem Steel steam turbines of 22,500bhp with double reduction gearing to a single propeller. Her normal speed was in the region of 21 knots, but she was capable of reaching 24 1/2 knots. Along with a few other members of this class of ten ships, the *Pioneer Commander* passed to the United States government in 1981 and was laid up in the National Defense Reserve Fleet at Beaumont, Texas, from 14 May that year. She was allocated to the Ready Reserve Fleet until 2001, and given pennant number *AK-2016*. As such she was made ready for disposal in 2009 and was sold to Marine Metals, Brownsville, Texas in 2012 for scrapping.

(the late C C Beazley)

In 1943 the United States Government Maritime Commission was planning a new type of fast, steam turbine-powered cargo ship, which would become known as the *Victory* ship. A total of 414 conventional cargo ships were built to three different designs. The most numerous were the 272 vessels of the VC2-S-AP2 design followed by 141 to design VC2-S-AP3, and finally the solitary VC2-M-AP4 type which was a motorship. *Victory* ships of the AP2 design were built at four separate shipyards, with construction commencing in the second half of 1944. The subject of this photograph is **Green Mountain State** which started out as **Flagstaff Victory**, a VC2-S-AP2 type. She was launched on 22 December 1944 and completed 29 January 1945 by California Shipbuilding Corporation at their Terminal Island yard in Los Angeles. She had a gross tonnage of 7,642 and an overall length of 455 feet. Her cargo space consisted of five holds and she was powered by a pair of General Electric Company steam turbines of 6,600shp. The **Flagstaff Victory** was sold by the United States Government in 1949 passing to States Marine Corp of Wilmington as **Green Mountain State**. By 1960 her owner was States Marine Lines Inc of New York, and this is how we see her arriving at San Francisco in March 1969. In 1970 she became **Reliance Solidarity** for the Hong Kong-based Reliance Carriers SA under the Panamanian flag, and was sold for scrapping at Kaohsiung in April 1971.

(the late George Lamuth [Marc Piché collection])

The American Export Lines, New York, operated a number of regular services to northern and southern Europe and Asia, from US north Atlantic ports and the Great Lakes region. Four vessels were constructed to US Maritime Commission design C2-S-A1 by the Bath Iron Works Corporation at Bath, Maine, and delivered in 1941/42 as **Exceller**, **Exanthia**, **Extavia** and **Exiria**. They were designed specifically for service with the American Export Lines and all four featured a counter stern. The **Extavia** was completed in October 1941 and was soon lent to the Ministry of War Transport, London and renamed **Empire Oriole**. During 1942 she was handed back, passing to the US Maritime Commission by early 1943 and reverting back to **Extavia**. The same year, she was converted to a troopship at Brooklyn and saw some service overseas before returning to her owner American Export Lines in 1946. The **Extavia** was powered by a pair of 8,800shp steam turbines supplied by Bethlehem Steel Co of Quincy and had a service speed of 16½ knots. American Export Lines was rebranded American Export Isbrandtsen Lines Inc from 1964, and both the **Extavia** and **Exiria** were sold for breaking up at Valencia in Spain in 1968. In this view we see the **Extavia** on the St Lawrence Seaway at Vechères in May 1965 on service between Chicago and the Mediterranean Sea. The remaining pair, **Exceller** and **Exanthia**, were scrapped in the United States in 1974/75 after spending fifteen years laid up in the US Government (Marad) reserve fleet.

(the late Captain John Low [Marc Piché collection])

LATIN AMERICAN FLAGS The New Waterway is the setting on 12 July 1975 for this view of the Argentinian-flagged tramp ship *Marvaliente*. She was trading for Compania Argentina de Transportes Maritimos "Ciamar" SA, and is registered in Buenos Aires. She was built by the Burntisland Shipbuilding Co Ltd in Scotland. Completed as *Baxtergate* she was delivered in 1962 to her owner Turnbull Scott Shipping Co Ltd, London. The 8,813grt *Baxtergate* was the last tramp ship built new for this fleet, although the secondhand *Arlington Court*, also of 1962, was purchased in 1964 and named *Southgate*, and was sold after just five years. The *Baxtergate*'s main engine was a 4-cylinder Doxford type of 6,640bhp in this case being built under licence by Hawthorm Leslie (Eng) Ltd. The *Baxtergate* tramped

worldwide until early 1971 when chartered to T & J Harrison who then renamed her *Mediator* for a few months until early 1972. On termination of the charter she very briefly reverted to *Baxtergate* before her sale. She was the last conventional cargo ship in the Turnbull Scott fleet when she became the *Marvaliente* in April 1972, for the owner mentioned above. The *Marvaliente* passed to Greek owners A Varsamis of Piraeus in 1981, and was renamed *Bravo Nek*. As such on 27 December 1981, she was involved in a collision with the Chinese-flagged freighter *Wu Men* (1975/9672grt) off the coast of Syria, and subsequently sank with her cargo of bagged sugar, loaded at Gdynia for Lattakia.

(the late C C Beazley)

The West German fleet of Norddeutscher Lloyd took delivery of seven 21-knot cargo liners named **Friesenstein**, **Hessenstein**, **Holstenstein** and **Schwabenstein** delivered in 1967, followed by the **Badenstein**, **Bayernstein** and **Sachsenstein** in 1968. When Norddeutscher Lloyd merged with Hamburg America Line in 1970, all seven ships were taken into the fleet of Hapag-Lloyd AG. The **Hessenstein** was completed in November 1967 by Bremer Vulkan at Vegesack with a grt of 10,146 and overall length of 530 feet. She was a part-refrigerated ship with five holds, nine hatches and partial side door access. She featured five electrically-driven cranes and eleven derricks, including a heavy lift Stülcken of 80-tons capacity. Accommodation was provided for twelve passengers and her main engine was an 8-cylinder MAN of 18,400bhp built by Bremer Vulkan. In 1974 she was sold to Ecuador Transportes Navieros Ecuatorianos (Transnave), renamed **Isla Puna**, and registered at Guayaquil under the flag of Ecuador. She is captured making progress along the New Waterway on 18 July 1975. Just over twelve years later she was sold to shipbreakers in Taiwan arriving at Kaohsiung on 25 September 1987.

(the late C C Beazley)

An interesting arrival at Swansea, albeit on the gloomy winter's day of 1 February 1971, was the small 14-knot motorship *Almar II*. She was flying the Uruguayan flag and most probably arrived from the east coast of South America. The *Almar II* was completed in November 1949 as *Saint-Clair* by the Chantiers Navals De La Ciotat shipyard at La Ciotat in France, as a 3,812grt refrigerated ship and part bulk wine carrier. She was delivered to Compagnie Générale d'Armements Maritimes, Bordeaux, and followed into service by the similar ships *Sainte Maxime* of 1950 and *Saint Ferreol* of 1951, from the same shipyard. The *Saint-Clair* was just 289 feet in length, and was powered by a 4,000bhp 8-cylinder Sulzer diesel manufactured by Forges et Chantiers de la Méditerranée. She had five holds which were served by eight 6-ton and a pair of 3-ton derricks. *Almar II*, purchased by "Saudena" SA Uruguaya de Nav (Flemar SRL) of Montevideo, was laid up at her home port on 27 February 1972 and ultimately broken up there in late 1978.

(John Wiltshire)

Swansea docks had strong trade connections with South America for many years and there was usually at least one vessel in port in the 1960s and 1970s loading cargo for this part of the world. Both British and foreign flag ships traded to South America, many of which would ship locally produced tinplate, for customers in Argentina, Brazil and Uruguay. The *Barão Do Rio Branco* was an attractive Brazilian-flagged freighter that had been completed in December 1963. She had a gross tonnage of 5,010 and was built at the yard of Companhia Comércio e Navegação Estaleiro Mauá Niterói, near Rio de Janeiro. She followed her sister *Barão De Maua* into service with Lloyd Brasileiro (Patrimonio Nacional) of Rio de Janeiro, and was joined by two more similar ships, the *Barão De Jaceguay* and *Barão De Amazonas*. All four ships had an overall length of 382 feet and were powered by a 5-cylinder MAN diesel resulting in a rather disappointing speed of 12 1/2 knots. In this view the *Barão Do Rio Branco* is noted at the far end of Kings Dock on 17 February 1970. She only ever traded under the Brazilian flag, and in the period 1973 to 1987, her owner was given as Navegação Mansur Ltda, Rio de Janeiro, and in a strange twist of fate, at the age of twenty-four years, she was broken up in Brazil by her builder. Her sistership *Barão De Maua* was even more unfortunate, as she caught fire in 1972, and was scuttled off Aruba.

(John Wiltshire)

Another Argentinian cargo ship was the Yugoslavian-built **Rio Corrientes**, which traded for Empresa Lineas Maritimas Argentinas and was registered in Buenos Aires. She is seen making her way along the New Waterway on 25 June 1977, and was one of a series of six similar vessels. The **Rio Corrientes** was launched in April 1962 at the yard of Brodogradiliste III Maj at Rijeka and delivered in February 1963, as the last of the class to be completed. This yard also built her sisters **Rio Carcarana** and **Rio Colorado** in 1962, while Brodogradiliste at Split completed **Lago Nahuel Huapi** in 1961 and **Lago Lacar** and **Lago Traful** in 1962. The **Rio Corrientes** has a gross tonnage of 8,482, a deadweight of 10,321 tonnes and an overall length of 516 feet. She was an attractive ship with a well-raked bow and a very rounded funnel shape, while her cargo space which comprised six holds, incorporated 72,000 cubic feet of space for refrigerated goods. Her superstructure extended both fore and aft to encompass No 3 and No 4 holds respectively (trunked-hatch arrangement), and her two main masts were of the bipod type. She had a 9-cylinder SA Fiat SGM main engine which developed 10,300bhp and gave her a speed of 16 1/2 knots. Most of this class was broken up in Argentina and the **Rio Corrientes** was dealt with at Ramallo by Talleres Martins, who took delivery of her in April 1986.

(the late Les Ring)

POWERED BY STEAM There follows a selection of steam-powered cargo ships. The small Turkish freighter **Nevsehir** makes a fine sight as she departs from Avonmouth on 1 September 1972. She was a steamship owned by DB Deniz Nakliyati TAS (Turkish Cargo Lines) of Istanbul, and had just turned twenty years of age. The **Nevsehir** was launched on 9 June 1952 as the **Dalheim** for Norwegian owner A/S Tank (Hjalmar Bjørge) of Oslo, and completed with a gross tonnage of 2,418 and overall length of 337 feet. She was a product of Norwegian shipbuilder Moss Værft & Dokk A/S, Moss, which also built two other similar vessels, **Bonita** of 1951 and **Bjorgsund** of 1955. The **Dalheim** was constructed as an open shelter deck vessel with three holds served by five hatches and accommodation for eight passengers. Power came from a 4-cylinder compound expansion steam reciprocating engine of 1,900ihp, and she had a speed of 11 knots. After a brief spell with her original owner, she became the Turkish-owned **Nevsehir** in 1955, with the two similar vessels **Bonita** and **Bjorgsund** spending most of their lives under the Turkish flag as **Kirsehir** and **Eskisehir** respectively. The **Nevsehir** was scrapped in Turkey at Aliaga during 1979.

(John Wiltshire)

46

Discharging timber from the Baltic at Ipswich on 30 April 1965 is the smartly kept steamship **Peter** of 1,565grt. At forty-nine years of age this fine looking tramp ship is coming to the end of her trading career, most of which was spent sailing for Scandinavian owners. She had a number of names over the years, but started out being launched on 6 November 1916 as **Harald** for Angfartygs A/B Gefle, Gefle, Sweden. Her builder was A/S Fredrikstad M/V, Fredrikstad, Norway, who installed their own triple expansion steam engine of 850ihp, and which received steam from a coal-fired boiler. She was recorded as having a speed of 10 knots and had two large holds accessed via four hatches, her gear consisting of just four 3-ton derricks. The **Harald** became **Eidsborg** in 1922 after being purchased by Norwegian owner A/S Forenede Rederier of Oslo. She was back under the Swedish flag in 1926 sailing for Nymans Rederi A/B as **Harriet** and registered in Stockholm. From 1929 until 1960 she sailed for two other Swedish owners, registered in Helsingborg as **P. L. Påhlsson**. Finally, from 1960, this veteran became **Peter**, as we see her in this view. She was now owned by Compania Maritime Peter SA (A Saarna) and registered in Panama, but managed by Ohlsonship Limited of Hull who had also operated **Ivar**, **John** and **August**, all of similar vintage, as well as **Kingham**, **Icaros** and **Weston**. **Peter** returned to Sweden to be scrapped at Ystad in November 1967 following a year laid up at Stockholm.

(John Wiltshire)

The **Zelengora** was a Yugoslavian-flagged tramp ship, and is seen moored on the Commissioner Buoys at North Shields on 28 July 1962. She had an interesting history, and was launched on 20 July 1943 from the yard of William Gray & Co Ltd of West Hartlepool as **Empire Nigel**. She was completed as an Empire B-type for the Ministry of War Transport (MoWT) and managed by Muir & Young Ltd of Liverpool. Her gross tonnage was 7,052 and she was powered by a 2,500ihp triple-expansion steam engine which gave her a speed of $10\frac{1}{2}$ knots. In 1944 she passed to the USSR under a lend-lease agreement as **Archangel**, soon becoming **Archangelsk**, but in 1946 returned to the Ministry of Transport as **Empire Nigel**. In 1947 she was sold to Fijian owner, W & R Carpenter of Suva who renamed her **Nandi**, but this was shortlived. In 1948 she was purchased by the Bristol City Line of Steamships Ltd (Charles Hill & Sons Ltd) and took the name **Bristol City**. Bristol City Line operated her until her sale in 1957, taking delivery of a new **Bristol City** in 1959 (see page 34). At this point she became the Yugoslavian **Zelengora** for Splosna Plovba of Koper. After a further fifteen years' service she was sold in 1971 to Compania de Navigation Portland SA (G J Marovic, Trieste) as **Taras** under the Panamanian flag, but arrived at Split on 6 July 1972 for demolition.

(Malcolm Donnelly)

The **Benvrackie** was named after a mountain in Perthshire and is seen arriving at London on 11 October 1975. She was a fine looking cargo liner built for use on a direct service from London and Rotterdam to Malaysia, Singapore and Hong Kong. She was launched on 25 November 1954 by shipbuilder C Connell & Co Ltd of Glasgow and completed for The Ben Line Steamers Ltd (Wm Thomson & Co), Leith in March 1955 with a gross tonnage of 10,302. Her propulsion was by means of a pair of double reduction steam turbines developing 9,350shp and built by D Rowan & Co Ltd. Steam was supplied by two oil-fired water-tube boilers, and her normal service speed was 16 knots but she had reached 18 knots on trials. The **Benvrackie** was 507 feet in length and had six main holds and hatches plus a small hatch on the poop deck, as well as a number of special tanks to carry vegetable oils and latex. Her superstructure was designed to include No 4 hold which was served by a pair of 5-ton electric cranes, a first for Ben Line. All her crew accommodation was located mid ships, and facilities for eight passengers were to be found in five cabins on the promenade deck. Connell subsequently supplied two further and similar vessels to Ben Line, the **Bendoran** and **Benlomond** in 1956/57. The **Benvrackie** lasted for twenty years passing to Taiwanese shipbreakers at Kaohsiung in December 1975. The **Bendoran** and **Benlomond** followed her in 1977.

(the late C C Beazley)

A large class of steam colliers was built in Poland at Gdansk by Stocznia Gdanska for the USSR. They were known as the Polish B31-type and eventually ran to eighty-seven vessels, entering service between 1952 and 1960. They were designed to carry coal, although some were probably used as tramp ships, while it is thought a few entered service with other Communist nations. The ship in this view is the **Povolzhe** and it should be noted that her name has also been recorded elsewhere as **Povolje**. Here she is on the New Waterway on 4 July 1979, inbound for Dordrecht to load for Klaipeda. The **Povolzhe** was launched as **Prawdinsk** and completed by November 1957, with a gross tonnage of 3,841 and a length of 355. Her machinery comprised a 4-cylinder compound expansion steam engine supplemented by a ZU Zgoda low pressure turbine, producing a combined output of 2,500ihp and giving the ship a speed of 11½ knots. The later vessels of the B31-type featured a modified superstructure and also had bipod-style masts, while in this view of the **Povolzhe** it can be seen that she still retains three of her four masts, but appears to have lost her derricks. Just over a year after this photograph was taken the **Povolzhe** was sold to Spanish shipbreakers at Villanueva y Geltru near Barcelona, where she arrived on 31 July 1980.

(John Wiltshire)

India Steamship Co Ltd, founded in 1929, was one of the oldest shipping companies in India, and in 1971 was still operating five *Victory*-type steamships in their fleet. Eleven new cargo liners were added to the fleet between 1955 and 1960, six of these being powered by steam turbine. The steamships and four of the motorships were built at Hamburg by Howaldtswerke Ham AG. These vessels which included the **Indian Renown**, **Indian Resolve** and **Indian Tradition** were regular visitors to the Bristol Channel, and the **Indian Splendour** is noted passing Battery Point in April 1975. She had arrived at Avonmouth with a part cargo from India, having loaded at both Calcutta and Cochin. She eventually sailed for Rotterdam and Hamburg, before making her way to Immingham to load back for India. The **Indian Splendour** was one of the steamships, and her machinery consisted of a pair of Howaldtswerke steam turbines of 9,860shp supplied with steam from a pair of oil-fired water-tube boilers. She was launched on 2 February 1957 and completed in the following May. She had a gross tonnage of 9,409 when operating as a closed shelter deck vessel, and her hull was strengthened for operation in ice. Her overall length was 508 feet and her normal service speed was in the region of 17½ knots. The **Indian Splendour** did not see further use with any subsequent owner and was scrapped in Bombay (Mumbai) in January 1980.

(the late Derek Chaplin)

The **Germania** makes a fine sight as she creates an almost perfect reflection in the waters of London's Royal Docks in April 1972. The Greek-flagged **Germania** registered in Piraeus was part of the Perikles Callimanopulos-owned Hellenic Lines fleet, who went out of business in 1984. She was launched on 19 December 1945 at the yard of Burntisland Shipbuilding Co Ltd in Fife and was built as an open shelter deck cargo ship. She entered service in 1946 as the **Kittiwake** for British & Continental Steamship Co Ltd of Liverpool with a grt of 2,016. Within her engine room was a triple expansion steam engine built in Glasgow by D Rowan & Co Ltd, which provided 1600ihp and gave the ship a speed of 12 knots. Two similar vessels were also completed in 1946 for this owner. They were the **Merganser** from the same shipyard as the **Kittiwake** and the **Lestris** completed by Hall, Russell and Co Ltd at Aberdeen. The **Kittiwake** assumed the identity of **Germania** in 1955, and remained in the Hellenic Lines fleet until 1977. At this point she was sold to Wadih Nseir of Lattakia, Syria, who named her **Hanan** and went on to rename her **Hanan Star** in 1979. Little is known about her subsequent history after sailing from Piraeus as **Hanan** on 6 February 1977, but she is thought to have been broken up in 1988.

(the late C C Beazley)

FROM BEHIND THE IRON CURTAIN The Finnish shipbuilder Wärtsilä Koncernen Crichton-Vulcan with its yard at Turku completed a freighter in 1952, which was subsequently delivered to the USSR as the *Archangelsk* (see also page 66 upper). This would form the basis of a standard tramp ship class, a further fifteen of which were supplied to the USSR, while a number were also completed for other customers including one for Czechoslovakia. They were introduced from 1955 onwards and early deliveries like the *Bratsk*, seen sailing from Eastham in July 1981, featured three pairs of king posts. Later examples had just one pair of king posts and also bipod masts, and the last pair delivered were the *Cherniakhovsk* and *Ljgov* in 1961. The *Bratsk* was launched in July 1957, completed two months later and registered in Leningrad. She had a gross tonnage of 5,518, and her hull which was strengthened for navigation through ice, was 457 feet overall length. Her distinctive split superstructure design incorporated five cargo holds served by nine derricks, which included one of 30-ton capacity. Her main engine was 9-cylinder Sulzer diesel of 6,300bhp built by the shipyard. The first examples of this class were scrapped from 1979 onwards, while two of them were actually sold for further service. Latterly recorded as being owned by the Baltic Shipping Company, USSR, the *Bratsk* was scrapped in the Soviet Union during 1982.

(Paul Boot)

The Polish government fleet, Polish Ocean Lines operated a large number of general cargo vessels of various sizes and many of these could be observed visiting ports in the Bristol Channel in the 1960s and 1970s. The **Legnica** registered in Gdynia was one of the smaller types and is seen arriving at Avonmouth on 24 March 1972 from Africa. She was one of a class of fifteen vessels to ship design B55, which also included the **Krynica** of 1958 and **Wislica** of 1962. The **Legnica** was launched on 10 December 1959 and completed on 30 June 1960 by the Stocznia Szczecinska shipyard at Szczecin. Her gross tonnage was just 3,351 and she had accommodation for four passengers. She was built to open shelter deck layout with five holds served by fourteen derricks including one of 30-ton capacity. The **Legnica** was powered by a 6-cylinder MAN diesel of 5,000bhp, located three-quarters aft, which gave her a service speed of 15½ knots. In 1980 she became **Giorgios**, owned by Grecomar Shipping Agency (D N Leventakis) of Piraeus. The end of her sailing days was reached in October 1983 when she arrived at Jamnagar in India for breaking up.

(John Wiltshire)

Rotterdam-based shipowner Van Nievelt, Goudriaan & Co took delivery of five unusual general cargo ships which were built at three different shipyards in the Netherlands. They were five-hold ships with the accommodation and machinery placed three-quarters aft. The forecastle was extended to 92 feet to encompass No 1 hold; while the poop deck was 98 feet in length and accommodated the superstructure and No 5 hold. The first ship was the **Alamak** delivered by Boele's of Bolnes, which also completed the **Alnitak**. "Gusto" of Schiedam built the **Alchiba** while the remaining two ships, the **Algorab** and **Aludra** were completed in 1960 by the Werf de Noord yard at Alblasserdam. They all had a gross tonnage in the region of 6,723 when built, and an overall length of 496 feet. We shall concentrate on the **Aludra** which had accommodation for twelve passengers and also featured 10,772 cubic feet of refrigerated cargo space. Four of the five ships mentioned above were sold to Norwegian owner Wilh Wilhelmsen for operation by Barber Lines, with the **Aludra** becoming **Texas** in 1969. Remarkably, this group of four were then sold to the China Ocean Shipping Company and the **Texas** became the **Li Shui** in 1973. She is seen here on the New Waterway on 12 July 1975. The **Li Shui** later became the **Li Tong** in 2004 and ended her days trading for Guangzhou Shipping & Enterprises Co Ltd, Guangzhou. It is most likely she was scrapped prior to 2010.

(the late C C Beazley)

Navigation Maritime Bulgare based at Varna was founded in 1892 and is still the major shipping fleet in Bulgaria in 2014, with a fleet of sixty vessels. In the 1970's Bulgaria began to expand its trade with the West and an early example of this development was the arrival at Cardiff docks of the small well-laden cargo ship **Burgas** on 3 April 1970. Other small Bulgarian ships noted trading to Cardiff were **Botevgrad** (1958), ex **Germa**, **Chipka** (a steamship of 1938) and **Sliven** (1961). The **Burgas** was a motorship built in Bulgaria by G Dimitrov Shipyard of Varna and was launched on 6 February 1958. She was of closed shelter deck layout, with three cargo holds, a gross tonnage of 1935, while her hull measured 303 feet in length with a beam of 45 feet. The **Burgas** was powered by a pair of 8-cylinder Schwermasch. Karl Liebknecht diesels of 2,000bhp, which drove a single propeller and gave her a speed of 13 knots. The **Burgas** had a sistership, **Varna** of 1957, which was wrecked off Portugal in 1968 while two other similar vessels were constructed by the G Dimitrov Shipyard. One was the **Mir** in 1959 for the USSR and which later became the North Korean-flagged **Pyeng Hoa**. The other was the **Jiskra** of 1962, which was built for Czechoslovakia and registered in Prague. As for the fate of the **Burgas**, all we know is that she was last reported sailing from Ravenna in November 1979 and reported hulked by 1982, presumably in Bulgaria.

(John Wiltshire)

The national fleet of the German Democratic Republic was VEB Deutsche Seereederei which had established itself fully by 1955, and by 1964 had grown to 111 vessels. Due to restructuring, on 1 January 1974 the title was changed to VEB Deutfracht/Seereederei. Between 1962 and 1966 sixteen X-type general cargo ships were delivered from the East German yard of Warnowwerft at Warnemünde, and all had a gross tonnage of just over 7,700. Two of this class the **Käthe Niederkirchner** of 1964 and the **Fiete Schulze** of 1966 were both losses when only around twelve months old. The **Wilhelm Florin** was completed on 2 April 1964 and had an overall length of 466 feet and a beam of 61 feet. She was powered by a 7-cylinder Dieselmotoren (DMR) engine of 5,850bhp giving the ship a speed of

14$^{1}/_{2}$ knots. As can be seen in this view of the **Wilhelm Florin**, arriving at Avonmouth from Port Sudan on a stormy 8 April 1972, the ships were built with six electric cranes and six derricks plus one of 25-ton capacity although, oddly, the cranes were later replaced by derricks. The **Wilhelm Florin** was renamed **Florin**, and placed under the Honduran flag, for her final voyage to the breakers, and she duly arrived at Kaohsiung on 5 December 1987 to be dismantled. Also of interest is that four of this class (**Edgar Andre**, **Ernst Schneller**, **Rudolf Breitscheid** and **Georg Schumann**) were converted into gearless steel products carriers in 1984/85 for use on a service between Rostock and Klaipeda.

(John Wiltshire)

The *Liberty* ship design came about as a result of WWII, and it was a cheap, simple and robust design that would be quick to build in large numbers. The ships were constructed in the United States and took the Maritime Commission designation EC2-S-C1, but had their origins in a British design. The *Liberty* ship was built at a number of shipyards across the United States including several newly-opened facilities. They had steam reciprocating engines of 2,500ihp and oil-fired water-tube boilers, but were not particularly fast vessels with a speed of between 10 and 11 knots. A total of 2,710 were actually built and after the war a good number saw further service with many being rebuilt often substantially. Somewhere in the region of thirty-nine *Liberty* ships were received by the Soviet Union direct from the United States on lend-lease agreements, while a small number were eventually purchased from other nations in due course. The **Bryansk** was obtained from the United States government in 1944, having been completed in May that year as **William E. Ritter**. She had a gross tonnage of 7,216 and was a product of the Permanente (Shipyard No 2) at Richmond, California. In this view the **Bryansk** is seen sailing from Durban during a voyage from India to Gdynia, and was the last *Liberty* ship to visit the South African port. The date is May 1974 and she was recorded as being owned by USSR (Far-Eastern Shipping Company) and registered in Vladivostok. She was broken up at Vladivostok during the summer of 1975.

(Trevor Jones)

LOOKING THE WORSE FOR WEAR This view of the Liberian-flagged *Mercury Lake* depicts a fine looking ship, the external condition of which has sadly been allowed to deteriorate. She is seen sailing from Cape Town in 1975 and is under the ownership of Mercury Shipping Co Ltd. She started out in 1952 as the *Straat Banka*, one of a pair of passenger cargo liners ordered by Koninklijke Java-China Paketvaart Lijnen NV (Royal Interocean Lines) of Amsterdam, her sister being the *Straat Makassa*. This shipping line operated a number of routes well away from Europe serving areas such as Java (Indonesia), Japan, South Africa, Australia and China with two routes calling at various South American ports. The *Straat Banka* was completed in May 1952 by N V Mch & Schps P Smit Jr, Rotterdam, with a gross tonnage of 9,138 and an overall length of 471 feet. Her passenger accommodation was for forty-six persons whilst her cargo space consisted of six holds. She was a single-screw ship powered by a 9-cylinder Burmeister & Wain diesel of 7,500bhp built by the shipyard, and had a service speed of 17 knots. The *Straat Banka* became *Mercury Lake* in 1971, while her sister *Straat Makassa* joined her with the same new owners that year as *Mercury Bay*. The *Mercury Lake* survived until 1978 when she arrived at Shanghai for scrapping.

(Trevor Jones)

At Cape Town in January 1970, the steam tug **T.S. McEwan** can just be seen attending to the Liberian tramp ship **Tolmi** on a voyage from Trieste to China. Unfortunately the ship's external condition leaves a lot to be desired, and it is known that she has had, and would continue to have, breakdowns and reliability issues for some time to come. The **Tolmi** started out as **Biographer** for Charente Steamship Co Ltd of Liverpool and was part of the T & J Harrison fleet. She was completed in August 1949 at the shipyard of Lithgows Ltd at Port Glasgow and had a gross tonnage of 6,915. She was the only steam turbine ship to enter the Harrison fleet in the post-war years, although the **Crofter** and **Forester** of 1951/52 had low pressure turbines to enhance their reciprocating steam engines. Her lines seem to predate her actual age and this may be down to the fact that at some stage her original funnel was replaced with this taller and more upright version. After just fifteen years' service she was sold in September 1964 to Angelicoussis & Efthimiou whose Anangel Shipping Enterprises subsequently grew into a major Greek fleet. **Tolmi** was initially managed by Pegasus Ocean Services Ltd of London and registered in Monrovia, but in 1969 she moved over to the Greek flag and was unfortunately plagued by generator problems soon after. After later running aground and suffering further breakdowns between 1970 and 1973, the **Tolmi** was eventually towed into Singapore. Due to neglect, she was declared beyond economical repair. The inevitable end resulted in a voyage to shipbreakers at Kaohsiung in January 1974.

(Trevor Jones)

The **Atlas Explorer** is a splendid example of a Norwegian-built cargo ship with split superstructure layout, and is seen here sailing from Durban in May 1974 following a two-month stay in port after a voyage from Singapore. By August 1974 she had been delivered to shipbreakers at Kaohsiung. She was ordered in 1940 from Framnaes M/V A/S, Sandefjord, as **Castleville** for D/S A/S International (A F Klaveness & Co A/S Lysaker) of Oslo, but was requisitioned in February 1941 by German authorities. Her launch took place in November the same year, and the ship was eventually delivered as the **Darss** to Die Kriegsmarine in December 1944. She suffered mine damage soon after this and was taken to Bremen for repair in 1945, being subsequently seized by United States forces and eventually handed back to D/S A/S International as the **Castleville**. With a gross tonnage of 6,091, she was an open shelter deck ship, with four holds including 11,330 cubic feet of refrigerated space. Unusually she was of twin-screw layout and her main engines were a pair of 7-cylinder two-stroke Sulzer diesels with a combined output of 6,650bhp at 145rpm. In 1963 the **Castleville** was sold to Rederi Ab Viking Linjen of Mariehamn, Finland as **Thor Viking**. In 1967 she became **Philippine Jasmin** for Lagona Navigation Inc (B Lim) of Manila and under Philippine registry, and finally as **Atlas Explorer** from 1969, sailing for Atlas Shipping Lines Inc (R Ramos), also of Manila.

(Trevor Jones)

The Panamanian-flagged cargo ship **Zak** is seen at New Orleans in September 1980 and is starting to show signs of neglect. She is just eighteen years old, but survived a little longer. She was of British origin and had been launched on 23 January 1962 as **Trebartha** for Hain Steamship Co Ltd, London. She was completed in May 1962 by her builder J Readhead & Sons Ltd of South Shields as a 10,148grt, 15-knot cargo ship with an overall length of 508 feet and a beam of 65 feet. She had five holds and her main engine was a 5-cylinder Sulzer built by the Wallsend Slipway & Engineering Co. In 1966 within the P&O Group, the Hain Steamship Co Ltd was merged with Nourse Line to form Hain-Nourse Ltd, London, to which the **Trebartha** subsequently passed. Her ownership changed to Peninsular & Oriental Steam Navigation Co with the next restructuring within P&O in 1972, and the **Trebartha** became **Strathtay** in 1975. She was sold in 1978 to Marikog Shipping Co SA, Panama, and managed from London by Marlborough Shipping Co Ltd (G P, J and P G Margaronis). **Zak** was laid up on the River Blackwater from 7 June 1982 until 8 September 1984 when she proceeded to load a cargo at Immingham for India. She arrived at Lianyungang in China on 9 January 1985 for demolition.

(John Wiltshire collection)

Norwegian-flag shipowner Wilh Wilhelmsen had for many years favoured the split superstructure layout for its cargo ships, and after WWII construction of this type of ship continued in 1946 with the **Talabot** a vessel of 6,104grt. The **Tennessee** was the first of a group of four to slightly smaller dimensions with a gross tonnage of around 4720, and an overall length of 429 feet. She was completed on 15 February 1949 by A/B Götaverken of Gothenberg and registered in Tonsberg. The **Tennessee** was an open shelter deck type 15-knot ship powered by a 7-cylinder A/B Götaverken diesel of 5,050bhp. She was sold by her Norwegian owner in 1968, passing to Kassiopi Compania Maritima SA of Panama as the **Kassiopi**. In 1970 she passed to Natalia Shipping Co SA (M G Sofianos), as **Evangelos M**. Sailing from Tarragona on 30 May 1978 for Dammam, she put into Aegion on the Gulf of Corinth in June 1978, and was placed under arrest and laid up as **Maximinus** for Interrnational Transaction & Shipping Co SA of Panama. Now looking a sorry state after six years in lay up, reportedly having at some point been renamed **Takis H.**, the ship has been caught on film off Piraeus between arriving from Aegion on 6 April 1984 and departing to the breakers yard at nearby Perama on 4 July. Although not obvious in the photograph, she has actually been renamed **Tiger's Tail** and is owned by the Roussos Brothers.

(Bernard McCall)

A visit to Avonmouth docks on 1 September 1972 produced this rather interesting little Greek-flagged cargo ship *Kerkis* which dated from 1947. She was owned by Poko Compania Naviera SA (Leonidas Pothas and others) and registered in Piraeus, and it is believed she was in port with a cargo of bulk oilseed from Karachi. The *Kerkis* was launched on 28 May 1947 as the *Bysanz* for well-known and much respected Norwegian shipowner Fred Olsen of Oslo. Her actual recorded owner was A/S Borgå, Oslo, with Fred Olsen & Co acting as her manager. She was completed in September 1947 in Gothenburg by Eriksbergs M/V A/B and had a gross tonnage of 2126. The *Bysanz* had an overall length of 338 feet, a beam of

44 feet and five hatches. She was powered by a 9-cylinder B&W-design diesel engine of 2,400bhp. In 1967 she went on charter to Cunard Line as the *Alsatia* and was put to work on the Cunard Lakes Service, which saw her trading in the North American Great Lakes for about a year. In 1968 she passed to her Greek owner mentioned above as *Kerkis*. She continued to sail on into 1976 by which time she had hopefully received some cosmetic attention. However, on 2 April that year, a fire broke out on board while she was on a voyage from Casablanca to Trieste. The *Kerkis* was subsequently noted beached and abandoned in the Bay of Milazzo, Sicily; and it is thought she later sank.

(John Wiltshire)

FLYING THE RED ENSIGN Houlder Bros & Co Ltd began the task of replacing wartime-built general cargo tonnage when in 1952 it took delivery of the cargo ship *Oswestry Grange*. She was an attractive ship of closed shelter deck arrangement that was launched on 3 October 1951 at the Tyneside yard of Hawthorn, Leslie & Co Ltd, Hebburn. She was completed in April 1952 with a grt of 9,406 and delivered to her owner Houlder Line Ltd, London, with Houlder Bros & Co Ltd as her manager. The *Oswestry Grange* was built for service between UK, the Continent and South America (River Plate), and had accommodation which was finished to a very high standard, with facilities for four passengers and two cattlemen. On the cargo side she had five holds and two deep tanks for the carriage of vegetable oils. For her size she was considered by some to be underpowered, and her 4-cylinder

Doxford main engine had an output of 3,780bhp giving her service speed as a modest 12½ knots. This lovely study of the *Oswestry Grange* was taken on 11 December 1971 at Barry where she had arrived to be handed over to new owners. It can clearly be seen that she has retained her white masts and derricks to the end, when officially they should have been buff. She shortly became the Greek-flagged *Dinos Methenitis* of Glyfada Seafaring Corporation, Piraeus and, following a year laid up at Clakis from 25 August 1977, she briefly flew the Panamanian flag for Seafreight Holding Corporation SA as *Dinos V*. The end came on 1 January 1979 when she arrived at Gadani Beach for scrapping.

(John Wiltshire)

The **Olivebank** was another example of Bank Line's fleet renewal programme (see also page 17). She was one of the seventeen ships completed by Harland and Wolff at Belfast, which commenced with the **Cloverbank** in 1957. The **Olivebank** was launched on 21 December 1961, completed on 12 April 1962 and registered in Glasgow for her owner Bank Line Ltd (Andrew Weir & Co Ltd). She was one of the last five completed which differed in a number of details. The closest sister to the **Olivebank** was the **Springbank** and they both featured a revised shape funnel and a 50-ton heavy lift derrick in place of the previous 25-ton derrick. The **Olivebank** had five holds and two deep tanks and was powered by a 6-cylinder Burmeister and Wain diesel of 6,700bhp built by the shipyard. She is seen on Gravesend buoys in April 1969, probably with a cargo of bulk raw cane sugar for discharge at Thames Refinery Jetty at Silvertown. The next series of ships for Bank Line consisted of eleven similar vessels, but larger at 15,900dwt, and again with orders being assigned to Harland and Wolff and Wm Doxford. The **Olivebank** was sold in 1978 to Good Harvest Marine Co Ltd of Taipei, Taiwan, and renamed **Golden Lagos** under the Panamanian flag. She was demolished at Kaohsiung during 1984.

(Douglas Cromby collection)

By 1955 the use of the triple expansion steam reciprocating engines in ocean-going cargo ships was becoming a rather outdated practice. Four late examples were delivered to Ellerman Lines Ltd to be used on their services to the Mediterranean. One of this quartet was the **Castilian** which was launched at the yard of A Stephen & Sons Ltd, Glasgow, on 24 May 1955. Upon completion her registered owner was Westcott & Laurence Lines Ltd, a company that Ellerman Lines had acquired in 1902. The **Castilian** was an open shelter deck design ship of 3,803grt with provision for two passengers. Her machinery consisted of a triple expansion engine manufactured by the Central Marine Engineering Works of West Hartlepool. This engine was enhanced by a low pressure turbine, with transmission through a hydraulic coupling and double reduction gearing to a single propeller shaft. The **Castilian** together with the **Anatolian**, **Almerian** and **Lancastrian**, spent various periods of time in the 1960s with *City* names or on charter to Cunard before being sold out of the fleet. Thus, **Castilian** was renamed **City of Peterborough** in 1963, reverting to **Castilian** in 1964 until renamed **Arabia** for deployment on their Cunard Lakes Service for two years from May 1966. She returned to Ellerman Lines in 1968 as **Castilian** once more, and was photographed on the Thames at Gravesend in September that year. She was the last of these four ships to be sold, passing to Maldives Shipping Ltd in 1971 as the **Maldive Freedom**. She was broken up at Gadani Beach during 1977.

(the late C C Beazley)

Currie Line Ltd was a shipping company with its headquarters in Leith and its origins could be traced way back into the nineteenth century as the Leith, Hull and Hamburg Steam Packet Co Ltd, and the title Currie Line Ltd was adopted from about 1940. The **Zealand** was a small single-screw ship that was built by the Henry Robb shipyard at Leith. She was launched on 10 November 1954 and completed ten months later as an open shelter deck type ship with a gross tonnage of 2,030. With accommodation for twelve passengers, the **Zealand** had a speed of 12½ knots and was powered by a pair of 7-cylinder two-stroke diesels of 2,620bhp built by British Polar Engines Ltd which drove through single reduction gearing and a hydraulic coupling to a single propeller shaft. She was originally advertised as being deployed on a service from Leith to Denmark, but it is known that she later operated from London to Lisbon with general cargo. The **Zealand** was built with an overall length of 270 feet, but in 1965 she was lengthened to 317 feet which gave her a new grt of 2,238. It is in her lengthened form that we see her passing Greenwich power station on the Thames in October 1968. Currie Line was purchased by Anchor Line Ltd in 1969 and the following year the **Zealand** was sold to Maldives Shipping Ltd and renamed **Maldive Envoy**. As such she continued to sail until late 1981, when she was sent to Gadani Beach in Pakistan for breaking up.

(the late C C Beazley)

By 1967 the Elder Dempster fleet stood at around thirty ships which included three passenger vessels. A series of five part-welded cargo ships were completed for the company by Harland and Wolff Ltd at Belfast between 1952 and 1956. The lead vessel in 1952 was the *Onitsha*, which was followed the same year by the *Obuasi* and, in 1955, the *Owerri*. The final pair arrived in 1956 as *Oti* and *Ondo*, and had no provision for passengers. Unfortunately, the *Ondo* became a loss after just five years' service. The *Onitsha* differed slightly from the subsequent vessels in that she had sixteen derricks which included one of 150 tons capacity, the others having just fourteen derricks. The *Oti* is named after a river that flows through Ghana, and in this view we see her sailing from Newport on the afternoon of 25 July 1969. She had a gross tonnage of just 5,485 and featured four holds with seven hatches, and also a deep tank for palm oil, located just forward of her machinery space. All five ships in this series featured a 5-cylinder Burmeister and Wain diesel engine of 3,750bhp built by Harland & Wolff, and the *Oti* had a service speed of 12½ knots. She was sold to Greek owners in May 1972 and became *Mimi Methenitis* under the Cypriot flag. She subsequently passed to other Greek operators again trading under the Cypriot flag but as Goldbeach Shipping Co Ltd, who named the ship *Goldbeach* in 1976 and then *Nicolas K* in 1979. She ended her days at Kaohsiung in December 1979.

(Danny Lynch)

The final four tramp ships built for Reardon Smith Line were regarded by many as the most attractive vessels of this type built post-war for any British fleet. They were fine looking 15-knot ships and were all products of the Pallion yard of Wm Doxford & Sons (Shipbuilder) Ltd, Sunderland. The **Devon City**, seen here sailing from Durban in March 1970, was the first to be completed. She was delivered to her owner Reardon Smith Line Ltd in January 1960 and was registered in the small North Devon port of Bideford. The others followed as **Orient City**, **Cardiff City** and finally **Houston City** in January 1963. The **Devon City** had a gross tonnage of 10,300 and five holds and was fitted with fifteen derricks which included one of 25-tons capacity. Her main engine was a 5-cylinder Doxford of 6,000bhp. All four

vessels in this series were sold in 1972, the last tramp ships in the fleet. The **Devon City** passed to Executive Venture Marine Ltd of Famagusta, Cyprus, and was given the new name **Executive Venture**. Just two years later she moved over to the Singapore flag as **Tong Beng**, initially for Kie Hock Shipping (1971) Pte Ltd, a company partly owned by Mr P T Lam; and then for Keck Seng International Pte Ltd from 1977, who later renamed her **Penta Y.** in 1978. Mr P T Lam, who had in 1978 created Ban Hock Shipping Management (Pte) Ltd, took over management of the **Penta Y.** in 1980. She passed to shipbreakers at Kaohsiung in April 1986, with the last of this quartet to survive, the former **Cardiff City**, making a similar trip later the same year as **Alpac Ocean**.

(Trevor Jones)

BIPOD MASTS The New Waterway is the setting for this view of the Yugoslavian cargo ship *Kapetan Martinovic* which is seen arriving at Rotterdam on 11 July 1975. After ten days in port she proceeded to Immingham and Newport to complete loading cargo for Arabian Gulf ports. She is a fine looking vessel but desperately needs some cosmetic attention to her hull. She was completed in November 1964 for Jugoslavenska Oceanska Plovidba of Kotor with a gross tonnage of 8,757. Both the *Kapetan Martinovic* and her sister the *Admiral Zmajevic* of 1965 were built at the Split yard of Brodogradiliste Split and had an overall length of 505 feet, and also featured tunnel side tanks for shipment of vegetable oils. Their distinctive bipod masts are clearly visible in this view and comprise eighteen derricks, which include one each of 25 and 50-ton capacity. In 1992 following the collapse of the Yugoslavian state, several Montenegro-based ships including the *Kapetan Martinovic* were transferred to Malta-based companies under the umbrella of Boka Ocean Shipping Corporation, nominally based in Liberia. Detained at Savannah in June 1992 by US customs due to economic sanctions imposed against Yugoslavia, she was moved to Charleston and then to Mobile from 9 June 1994. Presumably sold at auction, she resumed trading in 1996 as *Houston*, nominally owned by Texas Shipping Ltd, but it seems owned by the locally-based L Pappas and Don R Looper who renamed the ship *Kapetan Martin* following a grounding in May 1996. Two years later on 10 February 1998, the *Kapetan Martin* arrived at Alang, India for scrapping.

(the late C C Beazley)

In 1952 at Turku (Åbo) in Finland, the shipyard of Wärtsilä Kon Crichton-Vulcan launched a tramp ship, the **Equator**, for Finland-Sydamerika Linjen Ab (Finland South America Line) of Helsinki. She was sold to the USSR upon completion as the **Archangelsk**, and formed the basis of a class of sixteen ships. Meanwhile, in 1960 Finland-Sydamerika Linjen Ab returned to this yard for a pair of tramp ships to a similar design. The first of these was launched on 1 April 1960 as **Araguaya**, and was followed in 1961 by the **Aconcagua**. In 1965 Finland-Sydamerika was acquired by Finska Angfartygs Ab who kept both the ships until 1976. At this point the **Araguaya** and **Aconcagua** were sold to the newly-formed Pan-Arab Shipping Company of Alexandria where they were renamed **Abulfeda** and **Abulwafa** respectively under the Egyptian flag. The **Abulfeda** is seen in August 1991, having just emerged from the locks at Holtenau for a westbound passage of the Kiel Canal. She had a gross tonnage of 5,405 and was constructed to Ice Class 3 classification. Of split superstructure layout with five holds, her main engine was a 9-cylinder Sulzer of 6,300bhp built under licence by Wärtsilä Koncernen AB. Her sister **Abulwafa** was scrapped at Gadani Beach in 1987, but the **Abulfeda** soldiered on until arriving at Alang in India for demolition in November 1991.

(Bernard McCall)

During the 1960s Compagnie des Messageries Maritimes continued to operate a number of significant services worldwide. These included Marseille to Australia sailing out via Panama and returning via the Cape of Good Hope. They also sailed from northern Europe to the Far East and South America. Ten shelter deck type cargo liners were delivered between 1955 and 1958. Designated the F-type, they were generally regarded as being very successful ships. They incorporated a large Burmeister & Wain 8,300bhp diesel built under licence and were intended to operate at 16 knots. They put in up to twenty years' service with Compagnie des Messageries Maritimes, and the last pair were sold in 1978. All apart from one found subsequent buyers, this being the **Kouang-Si** which was sold to shipbreakers at Kaohsiung in April 1978. She was completed in June 1957 by Constructions Navales De La Ciotat, a yard which completed eight out of the ten F-types. The **Kouang-Si** was intended for use on the South African services and had extra refrigerated capacity and additional dedicated deep tanks to carry wine. She had a gross tonnage of 6,691 and five holds that were served by Halèn bipod masts. In 1977 Compagnie des Messageries Maritimes merged with Compagnie Générale Transatlantique to form Compagnie Générale Maritime (CGM), which in 1996 was acquired by Compagnie Maritime D'Affrètement to form CMA CGM, now the third largest container shipping line in the world based at Marseille.

(Trevor Jones)

Here we have another attractive tramp ship that was constructed in Yugoslavia, in this case for a well-known Swiss owner. The **Mindanao Sea** was launched on 31 July 1957 as **Cruzeiro Do Sul** at the yard of Brodogradiliste Split at Split. She was completed as yard number 144 in June 1958 for Maranave SA of Monrovia, a company owned by Suisse Atlantique Société d'Armement Maritime SA, of Lausanne. She had an overall length of 503 feet, while her cargo accommodation comprised five holds served by fourteen derricks. In October 1964 she was transferred to the Swiss flag and nominal ownership of Oceana Shipping AG of Chur, Bâle and renamed **Castasegna**. In this view we see her at Cardiff on 10 March 1973, where she has just changed her name to **Mindanao Sea**. Looking towards her stern the propeller turns, while the ship is still moored to the quayside. She later passed to China to be managed by front company Yick Fung Shipping & Enterprises of Hong Kong, and has been placed under the Somali flag. By 1976 she was trading for the China Ocean Shipping Company and was sailing as **Mao Lin**, registered in Guangzhou. Her last recorded voyage was from Japan to China in late 1982, and after 1985 her continued existence was uncertain.

(John Wiltshire)

D J Fafalios was a long-established London-Greek shipowner who hailed from the Greek island of Chios. Between 1969 and 1971 three new 17-knot tramp ships were delivered to Fafalios from the Pallion yard of Doxford and Sunderland Shipbuilding & Engineering Co Ltd of Sunderland. In order, they were named the **Finix**, **Feax** and **Faethon** and were 539 feet long ships with bulbous bows and a gross tonnage in the region of 11,500. Another Greek shipowner, Lyras Brothers Ltd, took three similar vessels in the same period which may be familiar to some readers as the **Iktinos**, **Iason** and **Ion**. There was a fourth Lyras Bros vessel, initially named **Ion**, which was sold before completion to T & J Harrison of Liverpool, becoming their **Benefactor** of 1971. Returning to the Fafalios ships, the **Faethon** was completed in May 1971 for Compania Viotia de Navegacion SA of

Chios, and had her engine and accommodation positioned three-quarters aft. The **Faethon**, like all the vessels mentioned, was powered by a 7-cylinder G Clark & NEM-built Sulzer design diesel, in this case delivering 11,200bhp. She was sold in 1987 to Kanica Lines Inc, Panama and renamed **Lake Michigan**, managed by Gleneagle Ship Management of Houston, passing to well-known Singapore owner Pacific International Lines Pte Ltd, Singapore in 1989 as **Kota Molek**. From 1995 she came under North Korean ownership, initially as the **Myo Hyang 3** and then **Sangwon**. It is as **Sangwon** that she has been captured on film at Singapore on 18 July 1999. Her owner is quoted as being Yuson Shipping Co Ltd of Nampo, and she passed to Indian shipbreakers just over twelve months later.

(Douglas Cromby)

CARGO SHIPS AROUND THE WORLD Here we have another ship with a slightly different end to her career. The *Khadijaan* was completed by Lübecker Flender-Werke AG at Lübeck-Siems in July 1956 as *Svolder* for Norwegian owner Aaby's Rederi A/S of Oslo. She was a five-hold cargo ship with an overall length of 478 feet and a gross tonnage of 8,858. The *Svolder* was constructed to operate in ice and her main engine was a 9-cylinder MAN diesel of 6,000bhp giving her a speed of 15 knots. In 1970 she went on a two-year time charter to Leif Høegh as *Høegh Svolder*, and was used on their West Africa service. She returned to Aaby's in 1973 as *Svolder* but was soon sold to become *Roman Emperor* for Greek shipowner Roman Empire Inc (Clipper Ships Inc) and was registered in Piraeus. She then

became the Panamanian-flagged *Khadijaan* in 1976 for Asio Atlantic Freighter Pte Ltd of Singapore. We see her heading up the Shatt-al-Arab waterway on 17 May 1980, bound for Basrah. She made one more round trip to Singapore returning to Basrah on 14 September 1980. At this point the *Khadijaan* was detained at the port, as Iraq closed the Shatt-al-Arab due to the war with Iran over the sovereignty of the waterway. Subsequently managed by Alam Maritime Ltd, London, she remained stranded at Basrah for thirteen years during which time she was declared a war loss. In November 1993 she passed to breakers at Alang.

(Andrew Wiltshire)

The *Pearl K.* was a typical Japanese-built general cargo vessel dating from 1960. In this view she is seen at Singapore early in the spring of 1981, soon after renaming, and is owned by European Navigation Inc of Piraeus, but registered in Panama. She was launched as *Philippine President Quirino* on 26 June 1960, at the Yokosuka yard of Uraga Dock Company which was a large and long-established shipbuilding company. She had a gross tonnage of 9,759 and was one of a class of six similar ships delivered from this shipyard, to the National Development Co, Manila, in 1960/61. Other examples included *Philippine President Magsaysay* of 1960 and *Philippine President Roxas* of 1961. The *Philippine President Quirino* was a six-hold ship with some refrigerated capacity and had an overall length of 510 feet. She had a speed of 18 knots and was powered by a 9-cylinder Sulzer-type diesel of 12,000bhp that was built by Uraga Diesel Kogyo. In 1966 all six ships in this series passed to United Philippine Lines Inc, and remained registered in Manila. In 1978 the *Philippine President Quirino* became *Galleon Pearl* for Galleon Shipping Corporation, Manila. *Pearl K.* was laid up at Ghent on 2 August 1982 and reactivated in October 1984, arriving at Huangpu near Shanghai on 25 January 1985 for breaking up.

(Douglas Cromby collection)

The early morning mist is just clearing on what promises to be a bright day at Cardiff on 10 March 1973. The Moroccan-flagged freighter *Atlas* is observed underway in Queen Alexandra Dock with assistance from local tugs. She was an attractive ship that was launched on 26 June 1959 at the Bijkers shipyard in Gorinchem, as *Argo Afaia* for Greek owners A Lusi, but was not delivered to them. She was eventually completed in December 1960 by a different yard, N Kon Maats "De Schelde" at Flushing as *Atlas* for Compagnie Marocaine de Navigation, Casablanca. She was a closed shelter deck type vessel with a gross tonnage of 10,392 and an overall length of 516 feet. Her layout was fairly typical for a tramp ship of this size, with five hatches and a variety of derricks including one of 30-tons capacity. Her main engine was a 6-cylinder Sulzer-type diesel of 7,800bhp which gave her a speed of 16$\frac{1}{2}$ knots. Some five years later in 1978, the *Atlas* was sold to Greek owners Yperion Compania Naviera SA (Golden Union Shipping Co SA). She took the new name *Alexandros* and was registered in Piraeus. As such she was laid up at Stylis on 12 January 1983 and eventually broken up at Chittagong in Bangladesh in late 1984.

(John Wiltshire)

Despite being a nation with an impressive maritime history, Portugal could not boast a particularly large ocean-going merchant navy. The fleet of Companhia Nacional de Navegação was based in Lisbon, being founded in 1881. In 1967 it operated just eleven vessels, with only three being less than fifteen years old. One of these was the Dutch-built 18-knot cargo ship *Beira* which, when completed in 1963, was the largest ship in the Portuguese merchant navy with a gross tonnage of 8,701. Her hull was launched by the yard of Arsenal do Alfeite at Almada, Portugal, and completed in May 1963 as the *Beira* by Nederlandsche Dok & Scheepsbouw at Amsterdam. When delivered she was classed as an open shelter deck vessel with an overall length of 530 feet with six cargo holds, incorporating some refrigerated capacity in No 3 hold. Her hatches were steel and of MacGregor single-pull design, while her cargo handling gear comprised derricks ranging from ten of 3 tons capacity to a single derrick of 60 tons capacity. In this view we see the *Beira* sailing from Avonmouth on 24 March 1972 assisted by the Cory tug *Falgarth*, also built in the Netherlands. In that same year the Companhia Nacional de Navegação fleet expanded when it was amalgamated with the fleet of Sociedade Geral de Comércio and eventually went out of business in 1985. The *Beira* had been sold during 1983, and ended her days with a shipbreaker at Bombay.

(John Wiltshire)

In 1971 the Scindia Steam Navigation fleet comprised around forty dry-cargo ships of which five were bulk carriers. Only three steam turbine-powered vessels remained and six members of the fleet were of British origin. One of these was the Yugoslavian-built *Jalagomati* which was launched on 24 August 1958 as *Siltonhall* for the account of West Hartlepool Steam Navigation Co Ltd. Her builder, Brodogradiliste III Maj of Rijeka completed her in December 1958 as yard number 452, and with the name *Jalasiltonhall*. This name change was brought about as she was to go on time charter to Scindia Steam Navigation Co Ltd of Bombay. When completed she had a gross tonnage of 9,056 and an overall length of 498 feet. She was constructed with five main holds and also had a deep tank for vegetable-type oils. The *Jalasiltonhall* had an 8-cylinder Sulzer Bros Ltd main diesel engine of 5,600bhp and a speed of 14½ knots. In 1963 the time charter ended and she was then purchased by Scindia and renamed *Jalagomati*. This is how we see her ten years later arriving at Cardiff on the late evening tide of 15 June 1973, at the end of a voyage from Kandla. After just under twenty-five years of trading the *Jalagomati* was sold for scrap, passing to breakers at Bombay in April 1983.

(John Wiltshire)

Time was running out for the Panamanian-flagged **Char Hsiung** which we find lying in Singapore Western Anchorage on 22 June 1980, about to sail for Keelung on her last loaded voyage, from Apapa/Lagos, Nigeria. She was built as a cargo liner and ended her days employed on services between the Far East and India and Africa for her owners Good Harvest Marine Co Ltd of Taipei, Taiwan. Following discharge, she made one final journey to the breaker's yard at Kaohsiung, arriving there on 8 August. In happier times she was launched on 25 October 1956 as **Tuscany** for Royal Mail Lines Ltd, London, and was the first in a line of four similar 13-knot ships; the others being named **Thessaly**, **Picardy** and **Albany**. All were constructed by Harland & Wolff Ltd at Govan, except the **Picardy** which was a product of their Belfast yard. The **Tuscany** had a gross tonnage of 7,455, and during her time with Royal Mail Lines she would have been engaged on their services from Europe to South and Central America and also Pacific coast ports in Canada and the United States. She was sold in 1970 to Federal Commerce & Navigation Co Ltd ("Fednav") of Canada becoming **Federal Hudson**, although retaining the British flag. Laid up at Halifax, Nova Scotia, in October 1972, her next owner was Goldtopps Navigation Co SA, and she was renamed **Golden King** under Panamanian registry for service between the Far East and India. She eventually became **Char Hsiung** in 1975, initially owned by Char Ching Marine and passing to Golden Harvest Marine in 1977.

(Nigel Jones)

In 1971 the Eastern Africa National Shipping Line Ltd, with its head office in Mombasa, Kenya was operating four freighters: **Harambee** of 1953 and three sisterships, **Uganda** of 1958, **Ujamaa** of 1959 and **Mulungushi** of 1960. They were deployed on a service that included Avonmouth, Glasgow, Hull, London and Liverpool, sailing to the East African ports of Mombasa, Dar-es-Salaam, Tanga and Zanzibar. The **Harambee** sailed under the Kenyan flag while **Uganda**, **Ujamaa** and **Mulungushi** flew the flags of Uganda, Tanzania and Zambia respectively. All three were purchased from the Danish fleet of Det Forenede Dampskibs-Selskab A/S of Copenhagen in 1968/69, and in which **Uganda** had carried the name **Colorado**. As **Colorado** she was built in 1958 by A/S Helsingørs Jernskibs & Maskinbyggeri of Helsingør as a cargo liner of 5,510 gross tons with six cargo holds and facilities for twelve passengers. The **Uganda** is seen off Newport on 9 January 1979. The Eastern Africa National Shipping Line Ltd was soon placed into liquidation and sold the **Uganda** in 1980. She was renamed **Kitmeer** for Sea King Maritime Corporation, Panama, and became **Al Medina** the following year for Amar Line Maritime Co Ltd and A A Q Bamaodah of Jeddah in Saudi Arabia. In 1986 she was renamed **A. Alamdar** for Ettrick Shipping Ltd of Gibraltar and was broken up at Alang in 1988.

(Danny Lynch)

The **Krasnyy Oktyabr** was one of a class of fast steam turbine-powered cargo ships built in the Ukraine for the USSR-Black Sea Shipping Co, Odessa. The initial four ships were built in 1959/60 and featured bipod masts. The **Krasnyy Oktyabr** was one of a further twenty ships completed between 1961 and 1964 that featured twelve 5-ton cranes and a pair of 60-ton heavy lift derricks. Most were built at Kherson but four were completed by I Nosenko at Nikolayev. The **Krasnyy Oktyabr** was launched in April 1963 and completed the following month by Kherson Shipyard with a gross tonnage of 11,206. Her length was 557 feet and her beam was 70 feet and she had six cargo holds. A pair of 13,000shp Kirov Works type TC-1 steam turbines gave her a respectable speed of 19 knots. She was built to operate in ice and these ships were regular visitors to the Great Lakes region of

North America. In this view taken on 28 May 1980, having discharged her cargo, she is seen sailing from Basrah in Iraq. Two of her sisters became stranded at this port later the same year due to the escalating hostilities in the region, and were eventually removed for scrapping. The remaining vessels in the class were elderly turbine ships which had no value other than scrap, and most were withdrawn for breaking up in the years 1984 to 1986. Following a voyage from Odessa to Kompong Som, Cambodia, calling at Singapore on 23 April 1986, the **Krasnyy Oktyabr** was briefly renamed **Krasnyy** owned by Zuru Maritime Co Ltd of the Cayman Islands, for the short trip to Kaohsiung for breaking up, where she arrived on 21 June 1986.

(Andrew Wiltshire)

We return to Malta once again in June 1978 and find the Danish freighter **Inger Skou** arriving in the Grand Harbour, and being escorted by the local tugs **St. Elmo** and **St. Lucian**. She was the third vessel in the Ove Skou fleet to carry this name, the previous bearer, a motorship of 1954, was wrecked in 1963. The subject of our photograph was completed in August 1964 as the sixth and final member of a class built in Denmark by Helsingør Skibsværft & Maskinbyggeri of Helsingør. Her owner upon delivery was given as Ove Skou Rederi A/S of Copenhagen and her sisters included the **Mads Skou** and **Kirsten Skou**. The **Inger Skou** had a gross tonnage of 6,460 and was powered by a 6-cylinder Burmeister & Wain of 6,500bhp diesel built by the shipyard which gave her a speed of 16^1/$_2$ knots. All six ships were sold by Skou in the years 1978/79, and **Inger Skou** passed to Greek owners Britannicus Maritime Co SA (K Fragoulis) of Piraeus in 1979 as **Damian**. Three years later she was sold to Panamanian owners New Haihung Navigation SA (Wah Tung Shipping Agency Co Ltd, Hong Kong), taking the appropriate name **New Haihung**. She did not do badly for a traditional cargo ship putting in just under twenty-seven years' service, and ended her days at Chittagong in March 1991.

(Alastair Paterson)

The Hansa B-type **Kathy Hope Maline** is an interesting vessel, and is seen at Montreal on 5 November 1967, heading for the Great Lakes and bound for Milwaukee. She has a substantial amount of deck cargo and there is evidence of a recent renaming on her bows. As the Swedish-owned **Virgo** she had been idle at Helsingborg from 4 March 1967 until emerging in June as **Kathy Hope Maline** flying the Liberian flag but owned by Constellation Navigation Inc of New York. Her building at the yard of A/S Helsingørs Jernskibs & Maskinbyggeri of Helsingør is understood to have been for operation by A/S af 6 Februar 1943 (Arne Kemp), but the hull was requisitioned by the German government for use by HAPAG of Germany as **Sandtor**. She was, however, launched on 21 August 1945 as **Egenaes**, and completed after hostilities had ended on 21 January 1946. Before entering service, the **Egenaes** was sold and traded as **Virgo** for Rederi A/B Iris (C H Abrahamsen) of Stockholm from 22 December 1945 until 1967, despite stranding in 1953 and again in 1960. Constructed to operate in ice, she was a 2,754grt steamship with a 4-cylinder compound expansion steam engine with enhanced power from a low pressure turbine. For over a year from 26 May 1970 the **Kathy Hope Maline** had been idle on the West African coast following a boiler breakdown, but in May 1971 became the Greek flag **Theodora K.A.** for Anco Shipping Co SA, Piraeus, and was broken up shortly after at nearby Skaramanga by Sidiremboriki SA.

(René Beauchamp)

ORDUÑA

THE TWILIGHT OF THE TRADITIONAL CARGO SHIP As the 1970s dawned, some ports in Venezuela, Peru, Ecuador and Colombia were still not prepared for containerisation. This was a region served by the Pacific Steam Navigation Co which was now part of the Furness Withy group. Their building programme for the 1970s, included three general cargo ships, ordered from Cammell Laird & Co (Shipbuilders & Engineers) Ltd for construction at Birkenhead. For delivery in 1972/73 they were of three-quarters aft layout and also capable of carrying a number of containers. The first ship was delivered in December 1972 as the *Orbita*, and was followed in 1973 by the *Orduna* and *Ortega*. This superb study of the *Orduna* arriving at Avonmouth was taken on 12 July 1975. She had been completed in March 1973 for Royal Mail Lines Ltd (Pacific Steam Navigation Co)

and was registered at Liverpool. The *Orduna* had a gross tonnage of 8,396 and a deadweight of 12,321, and was powered by a 15,000bhp Kincaid (B&W) oil engine. Her hull had four holds served by six separate hatches, and as can be seen the cargo handling gear comprised a mixture of 26-ton electric cranes and a pair of 10½ ton derricks. In 1982 she was renamed *Beacon Grange* and continued to trade within the Furness Withy group. In 1984 she passed to Cencargo Ltd, and was initially used to carry materials for building the Falklands Islands airport. As such she flew the flag of Bermuda as *Merchant Pioneer*. She was broken up in 1997 at Chittagong after four years trading as the *Jennifer R.* for the Great Circle Shipping Agency of Bangkok.

(Nigel Jones)

The **Meric** was the first of a series of six similar 18-knot cargo ships built at the same yard in Yugoslavia for the Turkish state-owned fleet D B Denez Nakliyati TAS based in Istanbul. She was launched on 14 February 1970 at Trogir near Split by shipbuilder Brodogradiliste "Jozo L Mosor" and was completed in August. The **Firat** followed in November, and the remaining four, **Aras**, **Dicle**, **Keban** and **Gediz**, were delivered in 1971. The **Meric** is seen close to home making her way along the Bosphorus at Istanbul on 2 May 1979. These six vessels traded worldwide, but were often to be seen in northern Europe and were also regular visitors to North America. The **Meric** had a gross tonnage of 9,042 and an overall length of 506 feet. She had five holds, bipod masts and was equipped with sixteen derricks plus a heavy lift, while her main engine was a 6-cylinder Sulzer diesel of 9,600bhp built in Poland by H Cegielski. All six vessels saw good service, although the external condition of some examples later on in their trading days often left a lot to be desired. Five of them were broken up between October 1996 and October 1997, with the **Meric** being dealt with at Calcutta in April 1997 following two years in the private Turkish ownership of Tempo Shipping and Trading. The last survivor was the **Gediz** which went for scrap as late as February 2004, after eight years' private ownership as **Baki I**.

(John Wiltshire)

In March 1957, after many years of British rule, Ghana gained its independence. In September that year the Black Star Line was established and four previously-owned cargo vessels were added to the newly-created fleet. From 1961 new vessels were purchased commencing with the **Offin River** and **Pra River**, a pair of cargo ships built in the Netherlands. The final additions to the fleet were four three-quarters aft general cargo vessels, which were built in South Korea. They were all completed in 1980 and delivered to Black Star as the **Volta River**, **Tano River**, **Keta Lagoon** and **Sissili River**, and were the first new additions to the fleet since the **Subin River** and **Klorte Lagoon** in 1969. They were constructed by Hyundai Heavy Industry Co Ltd at Ulsan and had five holds that were strengthened for heavy cargoes. They all had a gross tonnage of 13,004, and were designed to carry up to 500TEU containers, as well as general and bulk cargoes. The **Keta Lagoon** went on charter to Andrew Weir and Co Ltd as **Tynebank** from December 1980 until August 1981, after which she reverted to her original name. The first of this class to be sold was the **Sissili River** in 1993, but **Keta Lagoon**, seen here at Cardiff on 31 October 1994, lasted until 1998. At this point she was renamed **Ilion** for Medog Shipping Co Ltd under the Cypriot flag and with Greek managers. Later that year she moved over to Panamanian registry under the shortened name of **Lion** for Brentwood Commercial Corporation, sailing out of lay up at Falmouth on 10 February 1999 direct to Alang for scrapping.

(John Wiltshire)

The SD14 was a shelter deck general cargo ship, built to a standard design, and intended as a *Liberty* ship replacement. In 1966 Sunderland-based shipbuilder, Austin & Pickersgill was approached by London-based Greek shipowner Basil Mavroleon, with a requirement for two cargo ships to a cheap design. Two other Greek shipowners expressed a firm interest, and with a number of orders subsequently in place, the SD14 was born. It would have five holds and incorporate the 5-cylinder Sulzer 5RD68 diesel engine. The first SD14 was completed at A&P's Southwick yard in February 1968, and construction additionally took place at Bartram's nearby South Dock yard. The SD14 was subsequently built under licence in Greece, Brazil and Argentina, with a small number emerging from Robb Caledon

at Dundee and Smith's Dock on the Tees. The *Qing Jiang* was a fourth series SD14 that had been built at Southwick as yard number 1378. She was launched in January 1978 as the *Cluden*, and after a period in lay up was completed in the September for Matheson & Co Ltd (Indo-China Steam Navigation Co (Hong Kong) Ltd) with a gross tonnage of 9,327. The *Cluden* was sold in 1982 to the Chinese government (COSCO Guangzhou) and renamed *Qing Jiang*. This is the subject of our photograph taken in unusual lighting at Singapore on 27 June 2000, just minutes after the ship had dropped anchor. She was renamed *De Sheng* in 2007 and scrapped in China at Jingjiang during 2012.

(Douglas Cromby)

The Ivory Coast was one of the most prosperous agricultural nations in West Africa when it ceased to be a French colony, and gained its independence in 1960. In 1967 the shipping line Société Ivoirienne de Transport Maritime (SITRAM) was established, and by 1969 was operating a number of reefers. Further used tonnage was added to the fleet until 1977 when SITRAM took delivery of three purpose-built refrigerated cargo liners, capable of carrying a wide range of goods including containers. They were the **Yakasse**, **Yamoussoukro** and **Yopougon** and all three were named after cities on the Ivory Coast. The **Yopougon** was launched on 3 August 1977 at the Japanese shipyard of Mitsubishi Heavy Industry Ltd at Yokohama. With a grt of 13,022, she was classed as a cargo/container ship with facilities to accommodate 353TEU containers. The **Yopougon** had four holds and her cargo gear comprised five 25-ton and two 10-ton single-lift derricks, plus a 3-ton crane located aft, and is seen transiting the New Waterway on 8 July 1983. She became **Vincent De Paul** in 1992 under Bahamas registry for Société Navale Caennaise (SNC) and from 1995 was sailing for SCAC Delmas as **Vincent Delmas**. In mid-2000 she became **Dong Yang** in Hong Kong ownership, reportedly sold to Chinese breakers. However, she continued trading until sailing from Hong Kong on 18 December 2001 as **Hanyun No.1**, owned by Chang Yuan Shipping Enterprise, again of Hong Kong ownership. She was reportedly bound for Koror in the Republic of Palau and then never again traded. It is thought she was probably scrapped by 2012.

(George Garwood [John Wiltshire collection])

The last SD14 to be completed at the Southwick yard at Sunderland emerged in February 1984. Meanwhile, British Shipbuilders awarded a contract for two SD14s fourth-series ships to Smith's Dock Ltd at South Bank on the River Tees in 1982. They were for the Hong Kong-based Carrian Group which subsequently went into liquidation and did not take delivery. The two SD14s were sold in 1983, chartered to Empresa Navegación Mambisa (Government of Cuba) and renamed **Lilac Islands** and **Lotus Islands**. Smith's Dock built four similar SD14s for Cuba in 1986/87; the last examples of the SD14 built in the UK. They were the **South Islands**, **West Islands**, **East Islands** and **North Islands** and all were placed under Cypriot registry. The **West Islands** is seen here making a brief call at Santa Cruz, Tenerife, on 8 March 1990. Until 1994 she was operated by Empresa Navegación Mambisa, and subsequently by other Cuban government-owned concerns. She had a gross tonnage of 8,995 and deadweight of 15,136. Her sister, the **North Islands** was wrecked off the coast of Chile in 1997, but the remaining trio passed to Vietnamese-flag owners in 2000. The **West Islands** became **Phuong Dong 1** for Vietnam Sea Transport and Chartering. In 2011 she became **Sunrise 6** for another Vietnamese owner, Mai Mai Trading, and was last reported trading in 2012, although possibly since laid up or scrapped.

(Andrew Wiltshire)

The six *Fish* class vessels delivered to Bank Line Ltd (Andrew Weir & Co Ltd) in 1979 were amongst the last traditional cargo vessels to be built for service under the Red Ensign. All were built by Sunderland Shipbuilders Ltd, and the **Roachbank** was the first to be completed in January 1979 with the **Tenchbank** completing the series in November. New features included the raised deck around No 5 hold and the use of Velle single-lift derricks, while in the engine room was a Doxford 4-cylinder 76J4 of 12,000bhp. The **Ruddbank** was completed in June 1979 at the Deptford yard and had a gross tonnage of 12,214. She is seen here at Cape Town in September 1980. Her time in the Bank Line fleet was brief, being sold to the Vestey Group in 1983, and allocated to the Lamport & Holt Ltd fleet as **Romney**.

She took two further names within the Vestey Group, **Lairg** and later **Napier Star** in 1989, with registry being Hong Kong. In 1991 she joined two other former Bank Line ships in the fleet of Tamahine Shiping as the **Tamapatcharee**, and managed from 1994 by Andrew Weir & Co. She passed to John McRink & Co Ltd, Hong Kong, in 1995 as **Lady Rebecca**. In 1998 she became a training ship for the International Transport Workers Federation (ITF), and was renamed **Global Mariner** for a promotional tour of the world. On 2 August 2000, loaded with steel coil, she was in collision with a container ship at the port of Matanzas on the River Orinoco in Venezuela. She sank rapidly and was later cut up nearby.

(Trevor Jones)